Why I'll Never Hike
the Appalachian Trail

Why I'll Never Hike the Appalachian Trail

*More Writings from
a White Mountains Tramper*

Mike Dickerman

BONDCLIFF BOOKS
Littleton, New Hampshire

To Steve Smith and John Dickerman,
whose love and devotion for the White Mountains
greatly influenced me
in my early days of hiking.

Contents

Mount Washington and the Presidentials

Taking Issue

Peak to Peak

Mountain Nuggets

Acknowledgments

Writing and compiling a book like this is a true labor of love, and its completion would not be possible without the help and encouragement of many others.

Tom Hepner, publisher of *The Courier* and CEO of White Mountain Publishing, deserves first mention as he was the one more than three years ago who put his faith in me and allowed me to compile my first collection of hiking tales. Tom has been equally enthusiastic this time around, and once again has allowed me to reprint a series of columns that previously appeared in several of White Mountain Publishing's varied newspapers.

My longtime hiking pal Steve Smith has been a big booster of this project, and were it not for his infectious enthusiasm for the outdoors—something I contracted directly from him many years ago—it is doubtful this book (or any others I have completed) would have even been started.

Lincoln, N.H., photographer Robert Kozlow, Landaff resident Sally Boivin, and courageous peakbagger Larry LaBonte all graciously provided photographs for this book. Scott Cahoon of Passumpsic Publishing lent his computer expertise to the layout and design of the book. Likewise, Alan McIntyre, Nancy Collins, Roger Doucette and Doug Garfield Jr., all of Sherwin Dodge Printers, were extremely helpful in seeing this project through from beginning to end.

My wife, Jeanne, has been an invaluable supporter of this project, helping out in countless ways these past few months. I will always be thankful for her contributions.

Introduction

Hiking the trails, climbing the mountains, reaching the summits and taking in the distant views has been my passion for the better part of the last 15 years. I've been fortunate in that my health has remained good, my climbing legs have stayed strong, and my enthusiasm for the outdoors has never waned. When the mountains have called, I have always been able to answer. As a result, my relationship with the mountain world has strengthened over time.

My appreciation for the White Mountains of New Hampshire, I think, has always been in evidence in the regular columns and other pieces I have written while working for *The Courier* newspaper of Littleton, N.H.—a small town weekly paper serving the western side of the Whites. If reader reaction is an accurate barometer, then there's no question these mountain-related pieces have struck a chord with our paper's subscribers; both with those who live here in the White Hills, and those who live elsewhere (but wish they were here).

Although my job responsibilities for the paper are many, with the hiking and mountain stuff representing just a small part of what I do, my reputation seems to precede me wherever I go. I am looked upon as the guy who hikes and occasionally writes a newspaper story, not vice versa.

Ah, if only life were that simple in the newspaper business.

It's been more than 10 years since my first hiking column appeared in the pages of *The Courier*. Since then I've penned somewhere close to 300 such pieces, and have written about everything from peakbagging to summit weddings, and mountain triumphs to mountain tragedies. Almost from the start, readers have let it be known that they enjoy these journalistic endeavors into the mountains, so much so in fact, they planted the idea in my head of putting the best of these pieces into one single collection.

In 1994, I did just that, choosing my favorite columns so they could be compiled and published in the book, *Along the Beaten Path*, which, much to my pleasant surprise, was an unqualified success. The book you are now holding and reading is, for lack of a better term, the sequel.

Most every essay or article appearing here was previously published in one of three northern New Hampshire papers which regularly carries "The beaten path." The collection is a bit different this time around, though, as there are fewer recollections of my personal mountain journeys, and more meatier, issue-oriented and historical pieces.

Certainly I've grown as a hiker, columnist and reporter over the last 10 years. So too has "The beaten path." As I noted in my introduction to *Along the Beaten Path*, the evolution of this column—from a personal hiking journal to a more reflective, more serious outlet—is evident when comparing those pieces written seven or eight years ago to those that have been penned within the last couple of years. This evolutionary process has been good for me, good for the column, and I think good for the readers. It hasn't mattered whether I've been writing about a peakbagging puppy, winter life atop Mount Washington, or the latest mountain death; the public reaction has remained the same. Keep the words coming. There's nothing better than a good mountain tale.

On that note, I hope each and every one of you enjoys what lies ahead on this second journey along my beaten path.

Peaks and People

Mountain Survivor
Reaches Final Summit

April 5, 1995

As the rugged winter of 1993–94 gave way last April to the first days of spring, 57-year-old Lexington, Massachusetts hiker Larry LaBonte was relearning how to walk.

He had been in the hospital for more than two months by then, recovering from severe frostbite injuries to both his feet. He was wheelchair-bound, and still faced the very real possibility that he might lose some of his toes, and possibly his feet.

To someone who cared as much about hiking in the White Mountains as he did, the thought of being grounded, perhaps permanently, was sobering indeed.

Now move ahead 12 months to March 19, 1995. The day dawns sunny and reasonably warm (at least for a late winter morn), and the high peaks of the Presidential Range stand stark and naked against the crisp, nearly cloudless blue sky.

On the south side of Route 2, where the highway passes through Randolph on its way toward Gorham and Berlin, a band of nearly a dozen hikers take their first steps onto ancient Lowe's Path—the century-old trail leading from the valley up to the craggy Northern Peaks of the Presidential Range. Among the hikers is LaBonte, now a year older, a year wiser, and a just few hours away from the culminating moment of his hiking career.

As he and the rest of the group plod their way uphill, first along Lowe's Path, then along the Randolph Path, LaBonte can't help but think of the events of the past 14 months—events which forever changed him and his outlook on life.

"There are no winners, just survivors" is the line that leaps into his head time and again on this four-hour trek to the summit of 5,712-foot Mount Jefferson. LaBonte knows he is a true survivor.

Mount Pierce Misadventure

It was back on Jan. 22, 1994 that LaBonte and a similar group of winter trampers set out to climb two other White Mountains peaks, both southern neighbors of Mount Jefferson. The targets that cold, blustery Saturday were Mounts Pierce (Clinton) and Eisenhower, accessible via the Crawford Path, which rises gently out of scenic Crawford Notch.

As everyone in northern New England recalls, there was nothing easy about the winter of 1993–94, with its endless succession of snowstorms and bitter cold snaps. And for trampers like LaBonte and his intrepid team of climbers, all the hardships and toils of a true winter hiking experience were on display this particular day.

The team of five trampers, having slogged their way through mounds of drifted snow, eventually made it to the Crawford Path's junction with the Webster Cliff Trail, three miles from the highway and just few a rods from the actual summit of Mount Pierce. With conditions above treeline quite inhospitable, however, one member of the group, Henry Perles, opted to retreat back down the trail to Route 302, while the rest planned to continue on to the summit of the 4,310-foot peak.

LaBonte, an experienced winter hiker who had climbed all but one of the region's major peaks, also decided he'd had enough after a brief summit visit. Bidding three of his companions good-bye, he carefully made his way through the wind and fog back down to the Crawford Path, and began his descent off the mountain, leaving the treeless landscape near the summit for the sheltered spruce-fir woods scarcely 200 yards to the west.

But something went wrong almost as soon as the descent had begun. As LaBonte ambled along the upper portion of the trail, where scrubby trees give way to the featureless environs of the Presidential Range, he had trouble following the path he and the others had followed just a few minutes earlier. The snow-covered trail was rock solid, the result of wind-packed snow and several freezes and thaws over the last few weeks.

He looked left and right for signs of snowshoe tracks, or any other indentation which might reveal that humans had passed over the area. Finding none, he set a course downward, through the scrubby trees and into the white-coated landscape. Surely he would find the trail again once he immersed himself into the taller spruce–fir forest.

But down he kept going until it was obvious he was way off the track. And by then, he had no choice but to continue on his way through the pathless woods for nearby Mount Clinton Road, which would eventually lead him back to Route 302 and the Crawford Path trailhead.

Battling intolerable snow conditions, and exceedingly steep terrain, LaBonte decided to rid himself of the burden of carrying his loaded backpack. He also opted to ditch his snowshoes, which he could obviously no longer fasten to his discarded backpack.

Incredibly, he made his way down into a nearby ravine, and came across Perles, who had lost the trail in similar fashion to LaBonte. By then, however, LaBonte was laboring with every step in the deep, uncompacted snow. Also complicating matters was the fact he had mistakenly stepped into a hidden stream, and his Sorel boots had begun to freeze around his feet.

Perles, still with his snowshoes, forged onward toward civilization at around 4:30 p.m., while LaBonte followed slowly behind. Fifteen hours later, having spent the subzero degree night crawling on his hands and knees in Perles' footsteps, LaBonte was rescued from the winter wilderness by a team of Fish and Game officers and volunteer searchers. By then he was hypothermic and his feet and knees were frozen.

Frozen Like Fish

Two and a half weeks ago, as LaBonte and friends made their way toward Jefferson's rocky summit, the Massachusetts man knew he was in good company.

Of the people tagging along with LaBonte on the hike, many had spent countless hours with him over the last 14 months, though few of those hours were spent out on the trail.

Instead, many were spent alongside LaBonte as he recuperated from his frostbite injuries in a hospital bed in Littleton. In all, LaBonte spent 74 days of 1994 confined to various New England medical facilities; most of them at Littleton Regional Hospital.

"An awful lot of people, many on this hike, helped with my phys-

Larry LaBonte successfully summits Mount Jefferson in March 1995, a little more than a year after a hiking accident nearly cost him his two feet due to frostbite injuries.

ical and mental recovery," said LaBonte last week from his Lexington law office. "I owe these folks a lot. They have been wonderful friends."

Dr. Harry McDade, the Littleton physician recognized worldwide as an expert on treating cold-related injuries, recalled last week that LaBonte's condition was extreme when he arrived at LRH on January 23, 1994. "In the 30 years that I've been treating patients, he was one of less than a half dozen that arrived at the hospital with his extremities still frozen. It was a very unusual situation to deal with," said McDade.

It took 20 minutes for the emergency room staff to remove LaBonte's frozen boots from his feet, and another 10–15 minutes to carefully remove his frozen socks without damaging the skin on his feet. Even then, McDade still had to deal with two feet that he likened to "fish coming right out of the freezer."

Considering the damage to his extremities, LaBonte was fortunate that his feet were not amputated on the spot, as would likely have taken place at another hospital, where injuries such as his are rare, or at least rarely treated. McDade prefers a "conservative" approach to his medicine, however, and decided to put off undertaking any drastic measures without first completely assessing his patient's condition.

In the days and weeks following his admittance to the hospital, LaBonte was well aware that the unthinkable might still have to take place. "I made it clear that there were a lot of risks involved in the treatment I was giving him, and that he may very well lose both his legs from the knees down," said McDade. "Larry said 'Let's go for broke' and hope for the best."

Fortunately for LaBonte, no amputations were necessary, though he did lose a small portion of one of his toes.

Back On the Trail

Under the best conditions, no one, including McDade, expected LaBonte to be back on his feet and out on the hiking trail during the winter of 1994–95. "I told him maybe next winter (1995–96), but probably not this year," said McDade.

Up until last October, LaBonte was unable to wear any type of shoes on his tender feet, just sandals. Nonetheless, he attempted his first comeback hike in September, climbing to the summit of 3,129-foot Mount Crawford, his feet clad only in the summer footwear.

By October, said LaBonte, he was ready for shoes and even some off-trail hiking. He bushwhacked to a trailless peak near Shoal Pond, accompanied in part by UNH student Jeremy Haas, who a week prior to LaBonte's January misadventure had himself gained unfortunate national exposure as the brazen young hiker who led his friend and schoolmate, Derek Tinkham, to his untimely death on the southern slope of Mount Jefferson. For a short while in late January of 1994, Haas and LaBonte were both patients of McDade's at the Littleton hospital and had traded hiking war stories as they recovered from their winter wounds.

Undaunted by the onset of winter, LaBonte kept to the trail. First he climbed southern New Hampshire's Mount Monadnock, then graduated to the Whites, where he proceeded to reach the summits of Mount Cabot, Old Speck, Mount Hedgehog, East Osceola, Mount Adams and Mount Madison—with the exception of Hedgehog, all peaks exceeding 4,000 feet in elevation. By mid-March he was ready to take on Mount Jefferson, the lone 4,000-footer he had yet to reach in winter, despite three previous attempts.

"It was Dr. McDade who said to me, 'there are no winners, just survivors.' I was thinking about that all the way up the mountain," said LaBonte as he reminisced about the March 19 climb.

"At the risk of sounding pretentious, I dedicated this hike in my mind to Dr. McDade, for without his painstaking devotion, I would most likely be an amputee very remote from our beloved mountains; confined to life as a flatlander," wrote LaBonte recently in a letter to the Appalachian Mountain Club's Four Thousand Footer Committee, which this Saturday night in Boston will recognize LaBonte's completion of the winter peakbagging list at its annual meeting at AMC headquarters.

LaBonte's climb up Jefferson was also dedicated in the memory of 20-year-old Derek Tinkham, who LaBonte says, "was not as lucky as I" and whose tragic and needless death on the same mountain he was climbing "continually reminds us that 'there are no winners, only survivors' as Harry used to remind me on a daily basis."

"A year ago I was in a wheelchair, barely able to get around on crutches, never mind walk," said LaBonte. "The hospital bed in Littleton was my womb, my life.

"To stand on top of Mount Jefferson, on a day when the mountain gods blessed us with a warm sun, a bright sky, and little wind, was a great feeling."

And it was a feeling only a true survivor could completely understand.

Appalachian Trail Hikers Feed Off Their Experience

August 14, 1996

An item in a Vermont newspaper last week got me thinking about the trials and tribulations of long distance hikers.

The Associated Press story told of a Massachusetts backpacker who was asked to leave a Rutland, Vermont restaurant after gorging himself for three and a half hours on an all-you-can-eat salad bar. The man, 49-year-old Eugene Andersen, was backpacking his way along Vermont's famed Long Trail when he decided to hitch a ride into Rutland for the much desired restaurant meal.

Andersen, a community college student from North Adams, Massachusetts, was quoted as saying he wanted to "see food, savor food . . . I was there definitely to eat as much as possible and for as long as I was allotted."

It just so happened that on the day the account of Andersen's salad bar feast appeared in the paper, I was reading David Brill's 1990 book, *As Far As the Eye Can See*, which is his recollection of a 1979 thru-hike of the Maine-to-Georgia Appalachian Trail.

Brill, as it turned out, devotes several pages in the book to the same kind of food compulsion that apparently overtook Andersen when he stepped into the Ponderosa Restaurant last week.

"Consider that most long-distance hikers eat and metabolize as many as six thousand calories a day. After the first couple of weeks on the trail, when exertion tends to suppress a hiker's appetite, most [hikers] succumb to an incurable case of 'hiker's disease,' an affliction characterized by an appetite that simply cannot be satisfied," writes Brill.

Brill said food binges were the norm for AT hikers as they emerged from the woods after a week or more of wilderness hiking and soon found themselves in a town with grocery stores, ice cream shops, and restaurants (including those with all-you-can-eat offerings).

In Elk Park, North Carolina, related Brill, he and several other hikers visited a restaurant and like Andersen, chose to tackle the all-you-can-eat salad bar. As he recalled, the three arrived shortly after the restaurant opened on a Sunday morning, paid their three dollars, then consumed the entire contents of the salad bar "before the owner politely but firmly invited us to move on."

Appalachian Trail hikers, and to a lesser extent Long Trail hikers, apparently spend a lot of time thinking about food while they're trudging along the beaten path. Considering most of these hikers probably subsist primarily on noodle or pasta dishes, oatmeal, rice, gorp and other conventional trail foods, it's easy to understand why a quart of Ben and Jerry's ice cream or a fried chicken dinner would be so tantalizing.

"We became obsessed by food, talked about it incessantly, craved it, longed for it," wrote Brill in his book.

"I remember craving ice cream so much when I got to one trail town in the South . . . I was shaking. But I ate my ice cream," said another AT hiker, Rick Hancock, in the 1994 book, *Walking the Appalachian Trail* by Larry Luxenberg.

With the summer now winding down, and most northbound AT hikers in their fourth or fifth month on the trail, this is the time of the season when thru-hikers are daily passing through the White Mountains. You can usually pick a thru-hiker out in a crowd just by their ragged clothing, their generally unkempt appearance, and if they haven't been in town yet, either their strong scent, or the ravenous look in their eyes as they near the closest general store stocked with ample food provisions.

My experiences with thru-hikers have been limited over the years. Certainly I've run into my share of thru-hikers on the trail, especially right here in the Whites, where the AT passes over the region's most prominent and popular mountain peaks and ridges. But other than sharing a night or two in shelters with thru-hikers, I've never had the opportunity to really spend much time with them on the actual trail.

A few years back, while staying at Ethan Pond shelter near Crawford Notch, I did get to share the shelter with two thru-hikers. One was a tall, bearded Scotsman with torn up red shorts, scraggly hair, and the appetite of a horse. The other was Dan "Wingfoot" Bruce, the most prolific AT thru-hiker of all time. I met him on his fifth or sixth thru-hike of the 2,150-mile trail.

While I enjoyed visiting with the two hikers, especially the outspoken Bruce—who talked practically nonstop from the time he arrived at the shelter mid-afternoon to the time he continued on his way the following morning—my lasting memory of the night at Ethan Pond Shelter centers around food, of course.

Now I've never been very fond of freeze-dried food, but on this occasion I thought I'd test some of this type fare since the dinner had been given me recently by a local outfitters' store. Unfortunately it took only one or two forkfuls of the food before I realized the dinner wasn't quite what I had hoped it would be.

The Scotsman, who'd already gobbled down his evening rice dish, quietly took note of my dinner dilemma, and when he noticed I had all but given up on tasting any more of my beef-flavored dish, he decided he wouldn't mind taste-testing the meal himself.

Within five minutes, of course, the entire dish was devoured by the Scotsman, while I was relegated to topping off my meager dinner with a package of cheese peanut butter crackers and a handful of strawberry Twizzlers.

There are plenty of daily concerns that thru-hikers must contend with, including blisters on their feet, days and days of foul weather, and wild boars that roam the woodlands in the Great Smoky Mountains. None, however, appear more important than their neverending quest for food.

As Eugene Andersen, David Brill, and the Scotsman would probably attest, it's not so much what you eat on the trail, but how much, and how often. Even if it takes three and a half hours to get one's fill.

Taking Care
of the Old Man

August 9, 1995

Lifelong Landaff residents Arthur Allbee and Harry Hodge have a perspective on the Old Man of the Mountains that few men alive have today.

Allbee and Hodge, both 84 years old, were members of the 1927 crew that hiked to the top of the famous profile high above Franconia Notch to undertake repair work to its rocky crown. The work crew, led by legendary Rev. Guy Roberts of Whitefield, scaled the northern slopes of Cannon Mountain and hiked through the scrubby trees to the Old Man's forehead where they proceeded to repair a crack atop its forehead with a mixture of cement, wire mesh and sand.

Of the six men who took part in the fall 1927 work venture, Allbee and Hodge are the only two surviving members. Rev. Roberts, whose ties to the Old Man go back to the start of the century, passed away just a few years later, while crew members Carl Young, Robert Poor and Howard Bronson, all of Landaff, have also died.

Despite their advancing age, both Allbee and Hodge still look back with delight and pride at the work they did to help preserve the Great Stone Face. "We were young men back then . . . we felt like explorers," said Hodge in an interview last week at the McKerley Health Care Center in Franconia, where Allbee is now a full-time resident.

Rev. Roberts, whose persistence over a 10-year period led to the first work expedition (in 1916) to prevent the Old Man from crumbling away, was the preacher at Landaff's Methodist Church when he

Arthur Allbee, left, and Harry Hodge, both 84, recall their historic 1927 visit to the Old Man of the Mountain during a reunion in the summer of 1995.

approached the young men about aiding him in his repair work atop the Great Stone Face.

"We were all farm boys back then, and we were all pretty husky fellas," recalled Allbee. "Rev. Roberts knew who we were through the church, and he knew how many muscles we had."

The rugged hike up to the Old Man's forehead required men with plenty of brawn as each was called upon to lug 50 pounds of equipment and material. Allbee said his load consisted of 50 pounds of sand, while Hodge remembers carrying an assortment of items from chicken wire and pails to ropes and lunch.

"We were all teenagers, except for Rev. Roberts. I was 16, Arthur was 17. We were young and enthusiastic. It was exciting to be a part of this work group," said Hodge.

The group spent about three hours atop the Old Man doing repair work supervised by Roberts. Hodge said the project involved filling in a crack in the Old Man's forehead with cement, chicken wire and rocks. After mixing and pouring the cement, Hodge said each of the workers sketched out his initials in the as yet unhard-

Landaff residents Harry Hodge, Howard Bronson, Arthur Allbee and Robert Poor pose for a photo atop the Old Man of the Mountain during their 1927 visit to the Great Stone Face.

ened sealant. "I was told a few years ago that you could still find them up there. I can't confirm that anymore, but that's what I was led to believe," said Hodge.

In ascending the mountain, the workers hiked up what is now the Kinsman Ridge Trail from the site of the former Profile House. After reaching the top of the Cannon Cliffs, hundreds of feet above the actual Old Man, they had to make their way carefully down the mountain over the exposed rocks and through the scrubby vegetation.

"I don't think we'll ever forget the trip up the mountain. We each had such a load to carry, it was extremely exhausting," said Hodge. When the climbers did take time out to rest, they didn't dare take their packs off their backs. "It would have been too much work to put them back on again," he quipped.

Sitting atop the Old Man after completing their work, Hodge and Allbee remember eating lunch atop the mountain and then gazing out in wonderment at the marvelous spectacle before them. "There was a great big emptiness out beyond the Old Man. You felt that if you ventured too far to the edge and fell, you'd go off into outer space," said Hodge.

There is some confusion over when the work project actually took place. Notations on the back of photographs taken at the time indicate it was October 14, 1927, but Hodge and Allbee say it was a month earlier, in September.

"Originally Rev. Roberts tried to recruit us in the summer, but none of us could go because it was haying season," said Allbee, a lifelong farmer. It wasn't until mid-September that the crew was assembled and taken up the mountain. And a month later, several of the workers attempted a return trip to the Old Man for the benefit of a news film crew from Boston which wanted them to recreate the project.

The October trip never panned out, however, as cold, windy, and snowy conditions atop the mountain forced the teens and film crew to turn back once they got as far as the top of the cliffs. "It was so cold the lens on their camera froze," said Allbee. "We never did make it onto the big screen."

Allbee and Hodge said the ongoing efforts to preserve the Old Man can be traced to the perseverance of Rev. Roberts, who from 1906 to 1916 worked diligently to convince naysayers that something could and should be done to permanently save the Old Man from the debilitating ravages of Mother Nature.

It was in 1916 that Roberts and Edward H. Geddes, a granite quarry superintendent from Quincy, Mass., undertook the first major repair work on the Old Man, installing several turnbuckles which have since prevented the forehead boulder from slipping off the forehead proper and tumbling to the depths far below.

"Without Rev. Roberts, the Old Man probably would have fallen down by now," said Hodge. "He's the one who really saved the Old Man."

Rev. Roberts never returned to the Old Man after the fall of 1927, dying several years later. Like Roberts, Allbee and Hodge haven't made it back either, though they've been offered helicopter rides over the forehead by the Old Man's current caretakers, the Neilsen family of Plymouth.

If Allbee had his way, he said he'd see to it that Neilsen and his work crew were the only ones to trek to the Old Man's top. He's annoyed that a rock climbers' route passes close by the stone profile and that climbers routinely find themselves perched atop the Old Man. "They got no business going up there," said Allbee.

He also has little sympathy for the climbers who on occasion find themselves stuck on the cliffs just below the Old Man's chin—an occurrence repeated twice within a week last month. "They should put up a sign that tells these people that if they get stuck up there, they have to stay there. No one should have to go up and rescue them."

Allbee and Hodge realize their age prevents them from any rock climbing forays to the Old Man, though they joked last week they'd like to meet one another atop the Old Man "10 years from now."

Where or how Allbee and Hodge will be in 2005 is anyone's guess, of course, but thanks to their work and the works of many others since, you can be sure, at least, that the Old Man of the Mountains will still be in its proper place.

Allbee and Hodge, old men themselves now, helped see to that.

Women Hikers
Finally Get Their Due

November 15, 1995

Early hiking histories of the White Mountains are replete with tales of many great adventurers.

Starting with Darby Field's epic first ascent of Mount Washington (in 1642), these stories have primarily centered around male explorers who were often undertaking scientific explorations, or perhaps mapping out potential routes to the grand summits of the Whites.

Eighteenth- and 19th-century names that quickly come to mind when discussing early mountain expeditions include Jeremy Belknap and Manasseh Cutler, J. Rayner Edmands, Arnold Guyot, geologist Charles Hitchcock, Ethan Allen Crawford, and Edward C. Pickering.

History, unfortunately, has given short shrift to early female mountain climbers, who despite the noticeable lack of notoriety, did play an important role in establishing many of today's hiking trails.

The hidden role of women in early White Mountains hiking circles is, however, finally addressed in a new book published this month by Gorham-based Gulfside Press. *Mountain Summers*, compiled and edited by Peter Rowan and June Hammond Rowan of Randolph, tells the story of four women climbers who in the late 1880s took to the White Hills of New Hampshire with a fervor matching that of their male counterparts.

Mountain Summers traces the hiking exploits of these women through a collection of eloquent letters and diary entries written over a nine-year period beginning in 1878. The letters and dairies that appear in the book were discovered at a Woodstock, Vermont auction some 30 years ago by White Mountains memorabilia collectors George ("Joe") and Ann Kent of Rumney and Doug and Andrea Philbrook of Gorham.

According to the Rowans—who three years ago got permission from the Kents and Philbrooks to research, edit, annotate and eventually publish the collection—*Mountain Summers* gives long overdue credit to the women hikers of the late 19th century, some of whom frequently accompanied the more famous trail-builders and climbers of the day on their well-recorded mountain quests.

"Not a lot of information exists about women hikers of this era," explained June Rowan last week, "and that's what makes this book unique."

She said the letters are "written with a passion" that reveals the various authors' love and respect for the White Mountains. "It's obvious these women not only enjoyed the hikes and views for themselves, but also were willing to contribute something to everyone else, through their writing (in AMC's *Appalachia* journal) and in their trail-building."

Coinciding with the infant days of the Appalachian Mountain Club—of which the women in the book were members—the letters not only detail the many excursions into the hills by these hikers, but also reveal much about AMC's first days.

At that time, AMC members were devoting most of their summers to exploration and trail construction. "These women felt it was their duty to participate in each AMC exploration, no matter how tough the mountain terrain was," said Peter Rowan.

The principle characters in *Mountain Summers* are Isabella Stone, Edith Cook, Marian Pychowska and Lucia Pychowska, all of whom spent many summers in the White Mountains at various boarding houses stretching from Campton, north to Randolph and Jefferson.

Stone, from whose personal collection the letters and diaries originate, was an AMC member for 41 years and is generally regarded as the person responsible for the establishment of trails to Bridal Veil Falls in Franconia and Georgiana Falls in Lincoln. Her work with the club also resulted in many other trails being constructed in the Franconia Notch and Mount Moosilauke regions.

The Pychowskas and Cook hailed from Hoboken, New Jersey, where the Rowans write they resided "on a stately residence on the

Hudson River." Cook was an accomplished poet and author, and also dabbled in landscape painting. She frequently produced paintings and sketches of the White Mountains, which she would give to friends and relatives as gifts.

Lucia Pychowska was Edith Cook's older sister and the sister of noted White Mountains hiker Eugene Cook. Her interest in botany compelled her to make annual forays onto the Presidential Range to inspect and collect the precious alpine flowers that bloom in the arctic-like terrain early each summer.

Her daughter, Marian Pychowska, was a talented writer whose profound skills are evident in the letters she wrote to Isabella Stone, when she was just 18 years old. Her contributions to AMC in its early years have not gone unnoticed by the Boston-based club and there still exists today the Marian Pychowska Award, established to honor members who have contributed a high level of volunteerism and stewardship.

In *Mountain Summers*, the Rowans have neatly tied in the women hikers' exploits with those of other famous trampers of the day. A generous number of footnotes supply readers with invaluable background information on the characters and landmarks which are mentioned in the letters and diary entries.

"The biography information was the most difficult thing to put together," said Peter Rowan. "It took a lot of detective work to track down all the vital information we needed. We lived with this book, day and night, for three straight years."

Rowan believes readers of *Mountain Summers* can easily relate to many of the women's early hikes, "since a lot of the routes they describe in the book still exist today."

The editors also hope *Mountain Summers* will prove to be an invaluable resource tool for historians of today and tomorrow. "If it helps just one person track down that piece of the puzzle they haven't been able to locate, then we'll be pleased," said June Rowan.

One of the most precious nuggets uncovered by the letters is the tale of a hiker who loses his way while exploring the remote Pond of Safety in the Jefferson-Randolph area. There's another story of a springtime visit into snow-filled Tuckerman Ravine in which the trampers ponder the viability of sliding down the headwall. "It's made me stop and think a few times. Is the Pond of Safety story the first of an organized hiker search and rescue in the Whites? Is the reference to sliding down Tuckerman's the forerunner to today's skiing in the bowl?" asked June Rowan.

Unlike typical history books, June Rowan says, "The personal aspect of the letters" makes *Mountain Summers* different from any other book of its kind on White Mountains hiking. Those who read *Mountain Summers* will no doubt agree.

The Art of Tracking
(or Getting Intimate with Nature)

March 30, 1994

It is easy, when walking through the woods on your way to some mountaintop, to become so engrossed in one's effort, so involved in one's pursuit of making it to the top, that you forget where you are and what you are passing through.

A trail through the woods is more than a footpath to a specific destination. It is also an avenue that passes into and through the living and breathing world of nature and its many inhabitants. Unfortunately, in chasing after some peak or other backwoods spot, too often we pay little attention to what is there to see and absorb.

For Paul Rezendes of South Royalston, Massachusetts, looking but not seeing, hearing but not listening, is not something he can be accused of while tramping through the woods. You see, the fiftyish Rezendes is one of New England's leading experts in the art of reading animal tracks and sign, and a few hours with him in the woods gives one a much greater appreciation of the forest world and its many creatures.

A few weeks back, Rezendes made his way to the White Mountains to conduct a day-long workshop on winter tracking. For the better part of five hours, Rezendes, his wife Paulette Roy, and a group of 10 persons (including myself) took to the woods and learned—many of us for the first time—just what we've been missing all these years in our many forays into the forest.

As Rezendes describes it, "Tracking is the art of seeing." It is embracing an animal's environment. It is becoming intimate with the species and its ways.

"Tracking an animal is opening the door to the life of that animal.

21

Tracking and sign expert Paul Rezendes points out markings on a tree indicating bear activity in the area.

It is an educational process, like learning to read," writes Rezendes in his acclaimed book *Tracking and the Art of Seeing,* published in the fall of 1992 and regarded as one of the best books on the subject ever written. To date, more than 45,000 copies of the book are in print.

Rezendes believes strongly that by tracking an animal for an appreciable amount of time, one becomes "intimate" with its ways. "You can enter the animal's life . . . you can know where he's going even before he gets there," says Rezendes.

There is more to tracking an animal than simply following its footprints. While prints are certainly helpful in one's pursuit, there are numerous other clues in the woods that one may also follow. "You don't need to see a single track to find out what's in the forest. And you don't need snow," he advises. That's where the skill of finding and interpreting sign comes in.

An innocuous bent twig can reveal that a deer has been close by, browsing on new growth. A skunk-like scent in the dead of winter is a clue that a red fox has urinated nearby. And scratch marks on a trailside beech tree reveal that a black bear sought out food from the tree.

"The forest is always speaking to us," said Rezendes to his gathered workshop attendees. "But too often people aren't alive and awake in the moment. When we look, we don't really look. When we listen, we don't really listen. Something is missing . . . the intimacy."

The tools of his trade are few, consisting mostly of a tape measure, a notebook (and pencil), and his book. He will use the tape measure to accurately determine the gait and stride of any defined set or series of tracks. Then use the information gathered in his measurements to figure out what animal has made the tracks.

For more than an hour, much effort is expended on seeing, feeling, and measuring what are believed to be the tracks of a rare gray fox, which was seen by Rezendes and his hosts (Mr. and Mrs. Bill Adam of Landaff) a night earlier. The stride length and group length of the tracks are studied intimately. They differ somewhat from the track of a red fox, explains Rezendes, but he is convinced by morning's end that we are indeed on the trail of gray fox, though sign of red fox being around are also abundant.

Rezendes says when tracking an animal, one should look for consistency in the pattern of the tracks. "You don't always need to see a perfect track. But you need to see a pattern."

As we wander through the woods of South Landaff, Rezendes points out where a deer had been bedding down in the snow; the imprint of its front and rear sides quite evident in the snowpack.

His wife, meanwhile, introduces us to the practice of identifying an animal through sign left at what is known as a scent post. This is usually where an animal has left its mark by urinating. A small clump of yellowed snow is passed around to all so that we may find out for ourselves what deer urine smells like. It is sweet; not at all unpleasant. That smell will stick with us for the remainder of the day.

Later we track a fisher, which zigzags its way up a steep, wooded slope, apparently in search of prey. Its tracks lead us past a series of older, decaying trees scattered across the hillside. It is here that the fisher hopes to flush out his dinner; perhaps a mouse, or a squirrel, or some other small animal that utilizes the tree as its nesting place.

To our left, Rezendes spots a stand of trees debarked at their lower reaches by a deer, or a moose. By looking at the obvious scrape marks, he determines it was a deer that caused the scratches with his small, lower incisors.

Unlike early settlers of the Northeast, who used their tracking and sign skills to find and kill animals for food, Rezendes has another reason for tracking animals, and as he says in his book, it's for survival as well, but in a much different and humane sense.

He is a professional wildlife photographer, who makes his living by selling pictures of the wilderness and its inhabitants. To get the pictures he wants, he must find the animals first. And to find them, he often has to use his tracking and sign skills. He hunts, but only for the sake of getting the photograph. He eats no meat, and hasn't for more than two decades. To survive, he needs his pictures. And his pictures need the animals.

"Ultimately, tracking an animal makes us sensitive to it—a bond is formed, an intimacy develops," writes Rezendes. "We begin to realize that what is happening to the animals and to the planet is happening to us. We are all one."

Rezendes says tracking and reading sign "help us to learn not only about the animals that walk in the forest—what they are doing and where they are going—but also about ourselves."

For him, "This interconnection is survival knowledge and the true value of tracking an animal."

The Gentleman
of Franconia Notch

May 25, 1994

The tinge of a southern twang in his voice was the giveaway. One didn't have to be a rocket scientist or a Rhodes Scholar to figure out that Charlie Whiton was no North Country native.

He came to this part of the country some 21 years ago after an eight-year stint in the U.S. Navy. He was a native of Spruce Pine, North Carolina and at one point in his life thought he wanted to be a teacher.

The affable southern gentleman with a heart the size of a northern New England mountain found out quickly, however, that school life was not for him. So instead of standing in front of the blackboard, teaching readin', writin' and 'rithmetic, he took root in Franconia Notch State Park, where for two decades he was a fixture.

Whiton first worked in the Notch 21 years ago, serving as an assistant to signmaker extraordinaire Clyde Smith, who also happened to be his father-in-law. Next he became a member of one of Cannon Mountain's early snowmaking crews. Then he went on be a state park maintenance mechanic, a bus driver, and manager of the Flume attraction.

Eventually Whiton moved into the management office at Franconia Notch State Park, serving as administrative assistant for some six years. And this past winter, he was guest services manager for the mountain's ski area.

Co-workers at Cannon say Charlie Whiton was the ultimate "people person." You never heard a bad word spoken of Charlie, and you never heard him speak poorly of others either.

His sense of humor, his gentlemanly manner, his dedication to

25

Longtime state parks employee Charlie Whiton takes in the scenic winter vista from the summit of Cannon Mountain in Franconia Notch State Park.

his job, and his love for Franconia Notch and its enduring history and mountains made Charlie the most popular state park employee there.

"Franconia Notch was Charlie's life. He had a tremendous attachment to this place," said longtime fellow Cannon employee Damus Champagne last week. "You never knew when his days off were because he was always here, whether he had to be or not. And no matter what you gave him for a job, he went into it thoroughly, and he did it right."

"Charlie treated people like they were family. He had a way about him that was so easy going, so friendly. You couldn't help but like him as soon as you talked to him," said Amy Odell, a relative newcomer to the Cannon scene (at least compared to Whiton and Champagne).

He was the unofficial park "historian" said Odell, and through his casual conversations with parkgoers and tourists, she said Whiton had a knack for tracking down people who had stories to tell of life in the Notch years ago, and convincing them to send him items with some link to the area's past.

Whiton was also known as the "Voice of Cannon Mountain," and throughout northern New England his colorful winter reports on the mountain's snowphone were legendary in ski circles. It could also be said that Charlie never met a camera he didn't like, and he could usually be found in summertime lugging his 35mm camera with him wherever he might be headed. Of course sometimes he got more than he bargained when going for that "once-in-a-lifetime" shot, like the time a few summers back when while crawling on his hands and knees up the mountain to get close enough for a photo of a sunbathing bruin, he squished his way right through the bear's messy calling card.

Nonetheless, he proudly carried around his camera like a soldier carries his gun. "As long as he was outside, with his camera, he was content," said Odell.

In the week following Cannon's May 1 ski season closing, Whiton went into the hospital for heart surgery. Before he departed for the Hanover area medical facility, he cleaned out his office at the state park, taking things back to his Bethlehem home where he could comfortably work on things during his planned six-week recovery period.

On May 7, though, a day after his last recorded ski condition report was belatedly taken out of service, 50-year-old Charlie Whiton died suddenly and unexpectedly at the Dartmouth-Hitchcock Medical Center in Lebanon, leaving behind a wife, two children, his mom, and all those at-home work plans.

He also left behind a legion of friends, myself included, who will always remember Franconia Notch's southern gentleman as a person with all the values and qualities of a true North Country native.

Charlie Whiton was taken away from all of us far too soon, but he will remain with us and Franconia Notch for many years to come. And I suspect that if the Old Man of the Mountain ever utters a few words to those gawking up at him from the shores of Profile Lake, he just might speak with a tinge of a southern twang.

"Y'all don't worry about me," the Old Man will say. "Conditions up here are great, and they're only going to get better."

A Tramper's Life

A Green Mountain Odyssey

October 21, 1992

A teenage hiker once told me, "The best thing about backpacking is stopping at the end of the day."

Now I don't agree 100 percent with that assessment, for there are many other pleasures that I've always associated with backpacking, but certainly there's also a lot of truth to what this young tramper said. If you've ever tried your hand (and sore feet) at backpacking, you know just what I mean.

For the most part, I am a daytripper when it comes to hiking. I prefer a good night's sleep prior to any planned mountain adventure. I begrudgingly rise at dawn, to assure myself of an early start on the trail. Then at the day's end, long after I've exchanged my well-worn hiking boots for my Nikes or maybe my evening slippers, I sooth my aching body under a warm shower, then plop down in front of the television for a ballgame or an hour with Larry King, or maybe I slip under the covers with a good book or magazine. It's a good life, this daytripping life.

On rare occasions, though, I do venture into the New England wilds for a night or two out on the trail. And despite the discomfort of lugging a 40-pound pack on my back for what often seems an eternity, I actually enjoy these outings; though usually more so after the blisters on my feet have healed.

A few weeks back I took part in a most ambitious backpacking journey with five students from The White Mountain School plus their hike leaders, Barry Jones and Tim Felt. I joined the group in southern Vermont as they ventured along the Green Mountain state's famed Long Trail, which stretches some 265 miles from the Massachusetts border north to Canada.

The teen backpackers were participating in one of the school's monthly "Odyssey" adventures, which generally involve some type of extended masochistic outdoor activity. For this particular Odyssey, the hikers had taken on the herculean task of covering a 108-mile stretch of the Long Trail from Route 9 near Bennington to Route 12 in Barnard (a little east of Sherburne Pass and the Killington–Pico area). Their goal was to tramp this extended stretch of trail in a six day, five night period.

In order to get from Point A to Point B in their allotted amount of time, the group had to average 18 miles a day, every day. This would necessitate beginning their walking each day at or before sunrise and making camp for the evening sometime after sunset. It was an ambitious undertaking without a doubt.

In the week or two prior to the hike, I had consulted with Jones, WMS' outdoor program coordinator, several times, helping him put together an itinerary. It was during those meetings that he invited me to join his band of merry hikers.

Having backpacked only once previously this summer, I knew my body wouldn't be up for the entire 100 miles, so I chose to join in for just a day and half of trekking on Vermont's so-called "Footpath in the Wilderness." And that was only possible after finding out that Barry's wife, Angela, was also interested in joining the group for a day or two. Ultimately we arranged to trek down together and spot our respective vehicles 20 miles part, at the beginning and ending points of our segment of the hike.

Our original plan called for Angela and me to drive to southern Vermont on a Thursday afternoon, then hike south 3.5 miles to Story Spring shelter, where we would meet the northbound White Mountain School hikers on Friday morning as they passed by us on their second day out. All went according to plan that first day as we enjoyed a peaceful night in the shelter along with Angela's dog. When we awoke Friday morning, though, we were a bit antsy to get going ourselves, knowing we had 15 miles of trail to cover before day's end. So rather than wait at the shelter for the WMS group, we slowly ambled northward, back over the same terrain we'd covered the previous afternoon, and then waited for the rest of the pack at a U.S. Forest Service road crossing 1.5 miles away. And wait we did.

A White Mountain School student stops at a trail sign along the Long Trail and Appalachian Trail in southern Vermont.

Impatiently we hung around. Then finally at 11 a.m., the group managed to catch us. At that point, they'd covered 6.3 miles and still had another 13 miles or so ahead of them.

With rain and possible thunderstorms in the forecast, I meekly tried to convince Barry that instead of following the LT all the way up to 3,936-foot Mount Stratton, southern Vermont's highest peak, we cheat a bit and make a beeline for nearby Stratton Pond, a beautiful mountain tarn that is actually on the route of the LT, but reached in a roundabout way. The benefits of bypassing Stratton Mountain included four less miles of hiking, 1,700 feet less climbing, and the avoidance of getting caught atop the peak should an afternoon thunderstorm strike, as was predicted.

I got nowhere fast with my idea as Barry quickly pooh-poohed the suggestion that we do anything less than what the Long Trail guidebook suggests; this, even though the former route of the LT did indeed bypass the climb up Stratton. By 11:30 we were off and running toward the mountain, and as fate would have it, our hike soon turned into a soggy adventure.

The two-hour advance up the mountain trail saw us plod through rain and mud to the sheltered but soggy confines of the summit. We met just a couple of other hikers along the way; only two of whom were headed up the mountain like us.

Having hiked this section of trail twice before, I was the unofficial guide during the ascent. Unfortunately my memory failed to serve me when it came time to judge distances along the way. I caught a lot of deserved heat at the summit when my previous estimate that we were but three-quarters of a mile from the top proved way off the mark. All credibility was lost by the time we finally did reach the summit, a half-mile and 25 minutes later than anticipated. As the day progressed, I was reminded of my miscalculated guess over and over again.

As the weather was downright miserable by now, with wind, rain and fog enveloping the summit, we were fortunate that Stratton's mountaintop ranger cabin, generally reserved for the summit naturalist, was still open despite the lateness of the season (this being the long Columbus Day weekend). In fact this would prove to be our savior as the resident naturalist had the wood stove going and he was more than accommodating to us, welcoming us into his cramped, but comfortable quarters for a late lunch break.

Incredibly, both Barry and his wife knew the ranger from their working days with the Outward Bound program. This made for a homey lunch stop and an extended break from the rigors of the trail.

By 3 p.m. it was time to get going once again and soon we were back on the trail headed downhill, now toward Stratton Pond, some 2.5 miles distant, and then onward to the Green Mountain Club's William B. Douglas Shelter, some 7.4 miles to the north. This is where we intended to camp for the night.

Thanks to the rain, which had now pretty much subsided, the trail was slick and quite treacherous, but by the time we neared the pond, the rain had actually ceased and the temperature was a pleasant 55 degrees. We debated here whether to abandon our plan to continue north to the Douglas shelter. There are several nice shelters at Stratton Pond, any of which would have been fine for a night of camping out. But because the weather was now cooperating, we opted to proceed northward another five miles, knowing full well that the last mile or two would have to be covered under darkness as sunset was by then less than 90 minutes away.

The White Mountain School group, which included 17-year-old

Anthony Stevens, and 15-year-olds Galen Fulford, Peter Godt, Jason Frank and Eric Karr, more than held their own, despite being tired, wet, and hungry. They maintained an even walking pace and never tried to keep up with my steady, quicker march. Needless to say they appreciated any rest breaks along the way, even though there was a bit of urgency to continue walking as long as natural daylight still prevailed.

The final mile to Douglas shelter found us all proceeding forward with the aid of headlamps and flashlights. And despite some wet going the last half-mile to the shelter, we made it there all in one piece by 7:15; some 12 hours after the big group had begun its day some 19 miles ago.

The first hour at camp involved changing into drier clothes and socks, preparing and eating our dinner, and finding our way through the dark to the nearby spring. As I sat back and watched and listened to this collection of school kids—most of whom I'd never seen up until that morning—I could tell these guys were going to get their 100 miles and then some.

They were confident, yet hardly cocky. They seemed to know just what lay ahead of them, even though none had ever attempted anything like this backpacking trip before. They asked questions—lots of them—about what was in store for them the next day, and the day after that, and all the way to the end. It was all part of the psychological game one must play when partaking in such an abusive activity like long distance hiking.

I credit Barry and his co-leader, Tim, for keeping these kids in the proper frame of mind. Anything less than the commitment these guys showed and the venture could easily have flopped.

As I lay in the shelter that night, listening to the sounds of a passing thunderstorm, I worried about the following day's journey, which for me would entail a six-mile trek to a waiting vehicle. That six miles would be plenty, or so my body was already telling me. Meanwhile the real backpackers, these kids, slept the night away, oblivious to the raging storm outside and the 75 miles of walking that would confront them the next four days.

For this weary, out-of-shape soul, the best part of the trip was close at hand. For them, I could sense the best was yet to come.

Taking To the Rugged Trails

August 1, 1990

It seems every year at this time my hiking legs tell me they are ready for a challenge.

With black fly season out of the way and the summer hiking season at its midpoint, I am ready to take on practically anything the White Mountains have to offer in the way of hiking trails.

One year I remember taking a mid-July hike up the unforgiving Beaver Brook Trail to Mount Moosilauke on what would prove to be the hottest day of the summer. Another time, also in July, I tackled the challenging Madison Gulf Trail and ended up getting caught above treeline in a thunderstorm. Every year, it seems, I end up taking my harder hikes just as Mother Mature is throwing off her best heat.

This summer has proven no different as over the past couple of weekends Steve Smith, Creston Ruiter and I have taken on a couple of pretty mean mountain trails.

Two weekends ago, after more than a year of talk and little action, we finally hiked up into wild King Ravine on the northern slopes of Mount Adams, and then worked our way up the King Ravine Trail, renowned as one of the toughest but most spectacular trails in all of New England.

The trail, originally constructed by Charles E. Lowe in 1876, takes hikers from the floor of the boulder strewn ravine up to a spot known as the Gateway to King Ravine. In one stretch, less than 0.4 mile in length, the trail rises a stunning 1,300 feet in elevation.

We began our hike off Route 2 at the Appalachia parking lot, and from there took the Airline and Short Line trails to Mossy Falls, a nice little waterfall just below the ravine floor. After climbing several hundred feet more up into the ravine, we made our way over the rocky treadway to the base of the headwall, and for the next hour or more slowly progressed up the glacial cirque on what is really more of a hiking route than trail.

There was a lot of high-stepping from boulder to boulder, and few if any level spots where one could pause for a breather. I found the experience not unlike my summer expedition of a year ago to Maine's Baxter State Park and mighty Mount Katahdin, perhaps the wildest, grandest mountain in the East.

While the climb up to the Gateway was adventuresome, it wasn't until later in the day that we got a taste for what the Northern Presidential Range peaks are wont to serve up on a typical summer day.

Following a 30-minute visit to Mount Adams' 5,798-foot summit (second highest in New England), we were heading down off the cone when the first of two drenching rainstorms struck. The initial rainy blast came upon us so quickly and with so little warning that I didn't even have time to reach into my backpack and pull out my rain poncho. By the time I had located it and covered myself, I was already sopping wet.

Once the rain stopped, our waterlogged bodies proceeded over to AMC's Madison Spring Hut, where we managed to dry ourselves out some. But 40 minutes down the trail from the hut, a second rain squall blew in and again we got soaked to the skin. Naturally, it stopped raining just as we reached our vehicles back out at Route 2.

Our second recent outing, last Saturday, took us to Mount Passaconaway in the Sandwich Range. What made this trip so unusual was our choice to hike up the mountain on a trail that hasn't been officially maintained for well over 30 years. We decided to climb the 4,060-foot peak via the Downes Brook Trail (off the Kancamagus Highway) and by way of an old trail that follows the course of two slides which scar the mountain's northern face.

We had read about this route in older editions of the Appalachian Mountain Club's *White Mountain Guide*, but knew it had not been mentioned in any edition since 1955. As best we can figure, the slides, slickened by running water, moss, and lichens, were considered too hazardous for the average tramper, thus a decision was made at some point to close or abandon the trail.

Guy Waterman, author of several hiking books, including the recent mountain classic, *Forest and Crag*, had told Steve of this route last year. Guy said it was a spectacular way to climb Passaconaway. That was enough of an endorsement to convince us the trip was worthwhile.

The first part of the hike was easy enough as we plodded along the level grade of the Downes Brook Trail for just about two miles (or 50 minutes). At that point we began looking for signs of a rock slide that was supposed to be quite evident to our left. And it was.

The first mile along the slide was pleasant enough. The slide itself was extraordinarily wide in spots, and afforded us some pretty decent views northward toward the higher peaks of the Pemigewasset Wilderness. The route up the slide was also blazed, apparently by someone who has taken over minimal maintenance of the path. Cairns lined the way as well, though a few were disassembled and in need of repair.

The trail actually follows the course of two different slides. The first or lower of the slides was the easiest to follow, though care had to be used in places due to its wet condition, even in the middle of summer. The upper slide, which intersects the first at nearly a 90 degree angle—about a mile from where we departed Downes Brook Trail—was more overgrown, still wetter than the lower slide, and certainly narrower and more well defined.

The old hiking trail was in remarkably good shape when one considers just how long it's been since it has seen any regular maintenance. For the most part, the trail stays off to the right of the upper slide.

The final half-mile to Passaconaway's northern lookout near the summit was as steep a stretch of trail as you'll see in these mountains. Ascending through an extensive stand of spruce and firs, the trail climbed endlessly over slick, moss-covered rocks. A check of our topographical maps revealed that in the final half mile to the summit, we climbed about 1,200 feet up.

By the time we reached the summit outlook, less than three hours from the start of our trek, we were weary and ready for an extended break. We spent almost three and a half hours atop Mount Passaconaway before heading back to the Kanc in a roundabout manner by way of the Walden, Square Ledge and Oliverian Brook trails.

Both the King Ravine hike and the adventure up Mount Passaconaway were the kinds of hikes that make a tramper feel as though he has accomplished something. I guess that's one of the reasons I keep coming back to the mountains for more, even in the hottest days of summer.

Classic Climbs
in the White Mountains

June 19, 1996

Between now and the 4th of July weekend a team of students and faculty members from the White Mountain School of Bethlehem are undertaking an ambitious rock climbing expedition in the western United States and Canada.

In the course of their month-long adventure, the WMS group will be taking on 10 of the "Classic Climbs" of this continent. Their itinerary includes such famous mountains as Longs Peak and Halley Peak in Rocky Mountain National Park and Exum Ridge on the Grand Teton.

Now I'm not one much for perilous climbs that require ropes, pitons, and technical kind of stuff to get me where I want to be. I prefer keeping my feet firmly planted on the ground at all times. I mean, let's be real here. My feet have gotten me everywhere I've wanted to go so far. Like they say, if it isn't broke, don't fix it.

Since I have no interest in duplicating this school group's ambitious climbing agenda, I've decided that perhaps a "Classic Climbs" hiking series right here in the White Mountains would be more suitable to my ability and taste. Certainly there are dozens of hikes in the region that are considered "classic" by most every trampers' standards. It's really just a matter of figuring out which ones would be most appropriate.

Paring the list down to just 10 hikes is nearly impossible. For every climb added to my list, I've had to exclude one or two others.

In any event, here's one hiker's "Classic Climbs" itinerary. See you up on the summit sometime between now and Columbus Day.

CRAWFORD PATH   No listing of classic hiking routes in the Whites should leave off this trail, which runs from the top of Crawford Notch to the summit of 6,288-foot Mount Washington. Constructed in 1819 by the pioneer Crawford family, and known as America's oldest continuously maintained hiking path, this trail traverses the southern reaches of the Presidential Range and passes close by the open summits of Mounts Pierce, Eisenhower, Franklin and Monroe.

The trail is 8.2 miles long, and its terminus atop Mount Washington can be somewhat of a disappointment, since there's likely to be hundreds of other tourist-type folks at the mountaintop. The section of trail between Mount Eisenhower and Lakes of the Clouds is the most scenic. It's also the most dangerous in times of poor weather as there are no access routes into the valley between these two landmarks.

FRANCONIA RIDGE TRAIL   Next to the Presidential Range, this area of the mountains probably sees more visitors in a year than anywhere else. If you've ever walked the trail between mile-high Mount Lafayette and its southerly neighbors Mounts Lincoln and Little Haystack, you know precisely why this place is so popular.

The classic loop hike over these summits involves ascending Mount Lafayette via the Old Bridle Path and the Greenleaf Trail. Then it is south along the ridge over Lincoln and on to Little Haystack, and back down to Franconia Notch via the scenic Falling Waters Trail.

The ridge walk is highlighted by the traverse of the knife edge ridge between Lincoln and Little Haystack. It's not nearly as precipitous as Katahdin's stunning Knife Edge, but it's certainly worthy of a pass through.

MOUNT TRIPYRAMID LOOP   It's not the summits that make this trip a classic White Mountains climb. It's the ascent and descent routes that qualify this as one of the region's most spectacular hikes.

The Mount Tripyramid Trail, which diverges off the Livermore Trail out of Waterville Valley, leads over the north peak's steep slide, which rises some 1,200 feet in a half mile. It also passes over the south peak's loose, gravelly south-facing slide. Most hikers take on the north slide first, then cross over the mountain's triple summits before descending via the south slide.

This one's not for the faint of heart. Only the ablest bodies need apply.

Mount Adams via King Ravine   The Appalachian Mountain Club's *White Mountain Guide* aptly describes this route when it says, "It is very steep and rough . . . offering an overwhelming variety of wild and magnificent scenery."

The climb through this boulder-strewn north-facing glacial cirque is amongst the most rugged in all of New England. There are certainly easier ways to reach Mount Adams, New England's second tallest mountain at 5,774 feet, but none are this hike's equal.

Twin–Bond Range Traverse   For a true adventure into the heart of the White Mountains, no single hike tops this excursion. A traverse of the Twin Mountains and a visit to the three Bonds (Mount Bond, West Bond and Bondcliff) is a high elevation treat.

From the lofty heights of the ridgeline connecting the Twins and Bonds, you'll peer into nearly every nook and cranny of the lush Pemigewasset Wilderness.

It's probably best to undertake this trip over a two-day period, but it can be done in a long 20-something mile day.

Mount Washington–Tuckerman Ravine   Spring skiers know all about the ravine and its mystique. Summer and fall hikers frequent this area too. In fact, the route through Tuckerman's is the most popular way up to Washington's summit.

Unless you don't mind fighting with the weekend hiking crowds, it's best to tackle this route during midweek. Of course you may have to wait until mid-July before all the snow is gone and the path is clear of falling ice.

Mount Carrigain   Of all of New Hampshire's high peaks, perhaps none possesses as splendid a view as this 4,680-foot summit in the heart of the Pemi Wilderness.

Its central location puts this peak smack dab in the middle of all of the White Mountains' greatest peaks. The view from the summit observation tower offers peeks at more than 40 of the state's 4,000-foot summits. Only lofty Mount Washington boasts a higher summit count.

A hiker takes in the view of Mount Bondcliff as seen from the summit of neighboring West Bond.

The five-mile approach via Signal Ridge is fairly long by 4,000-footer standards, but every step is worth it, especially on a crisp autumn day when this "Watchtower of the Wilderness" is at its peak, along with the fall forest color show.

MOUNT WILLARD   There's nothing difficult about reaching this mountaintop at the north end of Crawford Notch. That's why this mountain is visited by thousands of trampers every year.

It's a great mountain for young hikers. It's a great one for older hikers. It's great for anyone with an appreciation of the mountains.

CARTER DOME–MOUNT HIGHT   The summits of these two mountains offer the best views anywhere of Mount Washington and the northern peaks of the Presidential Range. Arguably, no place offers a better perspective into Mount Washington's three great glacial cirques.

While it's easier approaching the two summits from the north, the true mountain explorer will scale the steep face of Carter Dome's south face from rugged Carter Notch.

Mount Hight has probably the better overall summit view, since it's treeless. Still, Carter Dome's summit offers worthwhile rewards of its own.

Owl's Head   I've got to be kidding, right? Afraid not. As any confirmed 4,000-footer peakbag artist will relate, the hike up remote Owl's Head is among the most memorable in one's quest for all the big peaks.

Unlike the other tall peaks, this one has no maintained trail to its summit. The view from the mountain's west-facing slide also offers a unique perspective on Franconia Ridge.

Never mind that it's an 18-mile round-trip hike to the mountain's wooded summit. This is one hike you'll never forget. Like it or not.

Bushwhacking:
A Way of Life Off the Trail

September 10 and 18, 1996

Early autumn weekends probably bring more hikers into the woods and onto the mountains than any other time of the year. Of course there are some very rational reasons why people choose late September and early October to don their Limmers and strap on the old backpack.

Try cool, refreshing weather, the brilliant colors of the foliage season, and the far reaching views in the clear mountain air—views that often extend over 100 miles from the higher summits of the White Mountains.

Certainly fall is my favorite time of the year for hiking. It's not by coincidence that I take a vacation week every year in September. Rather, it's so I can take advantage of the less humid air and strike off for summits that potentially will offer me the best views I can comfortably enjoy without having to ward off either summer's swarm of black flies or winter's biting cold winds.

The one down side to autumn hiking is that with so many people on the trail, especially on weekend days (which are generally the only times working stiffs like myself can find the time to climb), the opportunities for solitude in the mountains are practically nil.

Pass by any popular trailhead on a sunny, clear Saturday afternoon in late September and count the cars parked in the lot. In many instances, you can't even get to the lots since they're jammed-packed with vehicles and cars and trucks are spilling out onto the roadway shoulders. It's a guarantee that by the time the end of September rolls around, you'll find a hundred cars or more crowding both sides of Route 302 as its passes down into Crawford Notch. The same is true in Franconia Notch at the base of Mount Lafayette. Lord knows what it's like over at Pinkham Notch, where Mount Washington-bound trampers most assuredly take over at the Appalachian Mountain Club's Visitor Center on Route 16.

There are basically only two remedies that I know of that can ease the discomfort of the fall population surge on White Mountains trails. You can either take a vacation week like I do, and head into the mountains during midweek when the crowds are much smaller and the woods more woodsy so to speak. Or you can try your hand at some off-trail hiking, or bushwhacking, as it is commonly known.

The first option listed above is only good if one hasn't used up his or her vacation time back during that February ski vacation week, or the Fourth of July holiday week. If your meager allotment of time off from work has been spent, then bushwhacking may be all that separates an adventurous compass-led tramp in the woods from a mass gathering atop some cherished summit.

Bushwhacking, naturally, is not for everyone, nor should it be. If you're the kind of hiker who has a low tolerance for pain, or gets lost mapping out a road route from Littleton to Whitefield, then probably bushwhacking is out of the question. On the other hand, if you like taking part in challenging hikes, are knowledgeable in the use of a compass and map, and don't mind getting repeatedly whacked in the arms, eyes and legs while trying to negotiate your way through a thicket of hobblebush, then there's hope for you yet.

Identifying a destination, poring over a map for the best possible route, and then actually striking off trail and into the unknown wilderness can be a daunting, exhilarating and wearisome experience. The woods take on a completely different look and feel when you're traveling off trail, away from the beaten-down, blazed trails that one is accustomed to. Slopes suddenly seem steeper. Brook crossings become more challenging. Elevation gain takes on a whole new meaning.

When pursuing the New England 100 Highest peakbagging list a few years back, I had no choice but to learn all about bushwhacking since 18 of the peaks on the list were trailless at the time. With my longtime hiking pal, Steve Smith, serving as my mentor and mountain tour guide, I climbed to mountaintops in many remote corners of New England, passing over routes that Steve would usually plot out well in advance of our planned hikes.

Despite the many obstacles we as bushwhackers faced—including slippery, seemingly unclimbable ledges, impenetrable stretches of young spruce, and acres and acres of impassable blowdowns—each time we got off trail, we'd get where we planned to go without losing our way. Sure there were times when we weren't sure which way was left and which way was right, and on one occasion we got so turned around in the crowded woods that we hiked a half mile along a ridge before realizing we were going north when we should have been going south. But we learned from these misadventures and took that knowledge with us the next time we went bushwhacking. They were lessons well learned.

There's not enough space in a column like this to teach even the beginnings of compass and map use. But learning these skills is vital, as we found out earlier in the year when some downcountry hikers lost their way on Mount Tripyramid, even though they were outfitted with a high tech Global Positioning Unit and a cellular phone. If you have a map and can't read it, or if you simply choose not to bring a map along with you in the first place (as was the case with the lost hikers), you're lost before you even start.

The Appalachian Mountain Club routinely offers courses in bushwhacking and map and compass use. There are also a ton of books out on the market that teach those skills. I'll defer to the experts on which books are the best on the subject.

If you already have some basic bushwhacking skills and want to try your luck, start slowly with a destination that is easily reached. Certainly a bushwhack hike to a favorite backcountry pond or some minor 2,500-foot peak would be a good place to start. Take things slowly though. It's easier to get fouled up in the woods then you might think.

The Pains and Pleasures of Bushwhacking

Of course it takes a sense of adventure, a moderate to high threshold of pain, and a bit of craziness to voluntarily strike off into the mountains on a bushwhack peakbagging experience.

Off-trail hiking generally takes twice as much work and three times as much energy to accomplish the same things as tramping on designated, established paths. Often there is no reward at all for the extra effort, except for maybe a restricted view through the forested slopes of the mountain.

Roger Doucette holds up one of the remnants of the old fire lookout's post atop the northwest peak of Mount Hancock.

Hiking mountains is hard enough work without also having to deal with the inconveniences and pitfalls of an off-trail experience. Why is it, then, that some people thrive on bushwhacking to seemingly every nook and cranny in these hills?

Having partaken in a few bushwhacks of my own over the years—especially when I was in pursuit of summits appearing on the aforementioned peakbagging lists—I can attest to both the insaneness of these type of mountain pursuits, and the pleasure one gains from such ventures.

The insanity part is obvious when one considers what goes into a major bushwhacking trek, such as an ascent of remote Vose Spur in the Pemi Wilderness, or a visit to the seldom explored recesses of the Little River valley in Bethlehem and Twin Mountain.

While normal gangs of hikers are wheezing their way up graded paths maintained by the Forest Service or the highly efficient trail crews of the Appalachian Mountain Club, bushwhackers are fighting their way under, over or around a stand of dead trees leveled by some recent windstorm.

The on-trail hiker, though perhaps winded by the steady uphill grade of the footpath, stops every 10 or 15 minutes to catch his or her breath. The bushwhacker may need that same 10 or 15 minutes to move 100 feet or less upwards as his way is blocked by windfalls, or thick, scrubby patches of young spruce, or maybe a seemingly unclimbable rock ledge that appears out of nowhere along the otherwise heavily forested slope.

To the hiker making his way along the Twinway from AMC's Zealand Falls Hut to the summit of Mount Zealand, it's a relatively painless two-hour tramp up the mountain's eastern ridgeline. To the bushwhacker headed for the summit through the trailless upper reaches of the Little River valley, and along Zealand's claustrophobic north ridge, it will take five or six hours of laborious walking, crawling and sweating to get there.

Same place. Different route. And twice to three times the aggravation.

But enough said about the negatives of bushwhacking. What about the positives? There are some, aren't there?

The answer is yes.

The aforementioned spirit of adventure is what drives hikers to make their way off the beaten path and head into the unknown. Bushwhacking enthusiasts are usually driven by the unquenchable thirst for another peak on some list, or simply a desire to reach a mountaintop, or a ledge, or maybe some backcountry pond by means that normal hikers wouldn't even consider.

The New England 100 Highest peakbagging list got me hooked on off-trail hiking a decade ago. I knew if I was truly serious about climbing to the summit of New England's 100 highest peaks, I'd have to venture off trail a few times, since many of the listed peaks had no maintained trails to the summits. Initially I dreaded the prospect of tackling 3,870-foot Vose Spur (a spur peak of Mount Carrigain) without the aid of a recognizable mountain path, since I'd heard all these horror stories from other hikers about the difficulties involved in attaining its wooded summit.

I entered the bushwhacking phase of my hiking career with a decent knowledge of orienteering and map reading. I knew, however,

I'd have to learn more quickly if I hoped to be successful in reaching all the listed peaks.

Under the guidance of my longtime hiking buddy Steve Smith, who, incidentally, is rarely ever found on-trail anymore (since he's always bushwhacking his way through the Whites), I gradually learned how to get around in the mountains without the aid of a guidebook, or direction signs, or a well maintained footway. And when I finished off the 100 Highest list six years ago, I kept on striking off into the wild, though not nearly as often as Steve or the other converts he has brainwashed into joining him nearly every weekend of the year.

The real motivation behind bushwhacking is to get where no one—or at least very few people—have ever gotten before. In the White Mountains, where public roadways make every mountaintop and river valley easily accessible, there is no place in the region that one can't walk to in a day. I know that. You know that. So do thousands and thousands of other hikers. That's why our trails seem clogged with hikers far too often in the busier times of the year, like autumn.

The accessibility factor can work in a bushwhacker's favor, though. If it's possible to hike by trail 9.5 miles to Mount Bondcliff. Then it's also possible to hike off-trail to other hidden gems in the mountains; even if its only a spruce-clad 2,200-foot summit deep in the Pemi Wilderness, or a small slide on the west slopes of uninviting Mount Hitchcock.

As I found out several years back, it's not out of the question, especially in the long days of summer, to strike off on a six-mile (one-way) bushwhack hike to pristine Carrigain Pond—perhaps the remotest, most stunningly beautiful tarn in the White Mountains—and still be home in time for a late dinner.

Some of my most memorable hikes have been those taken off-trail. In May of 1995, for instance, I took part in a hike to the northwest summit of Mount Hancock; a mountaintop which 50 years ago served as post for a fire outlook. Our trek included ascending a wide, one-third mile long slide on the mountain's west-facing slope. The slide was a landmark Steve and I had identified as the best route to the summit during a trip up onto the Bond Range six or seven years earlier.

Besides being treated to views few hikers ever attain, we also got to survey the summit remains of the lookout's post, and even toyed with the idea of following the old phone line back down off the mountain (as previous visitors had told me they'd done). Instead, we struck off through the pathless woods to the summit of North Hancock, where we knew we'd find a maintained trail that would get us back out to our car parked off the Kancamagus Highway.

It is successful explorations like the Hancock excursion that motivate bushwhackers to get off the trail; not some hidden desire for pain, aggravation, or sheer exhaustion.

Bushwhacking, while not for everyone, fills a void that normal trail hiking can't or no longer fulfills. Yes, you have to be a bit of a masochist to bushwhack. But the pain is usually exceeded by the pleasure, and it's the pleasures of off-trail hiking that are the true reward.

Why I'll Never Hike
the Appalachian Trail

March 19, 1997

The official start to spring arrives this weekend and while it will most certainly be a few weeks before the season really settles in here in the North Country, the changing of the seasons is probably in full evidence already atop Springer Mountain in Georgia.

It is here, atop this 3,782-foot summit in the Chattahoochee National Forest, that hikers are starting out on their 2,100-plus mile trek northward along the famed Appalachian Trail. Five months from now, and approximately 5 million steps later (give or take a few thousand strides), these same trampers, or at least a small percentage of them, will reach northern Maine's Mount Katahdin.

Hiking the Appalachian Trail end-to-end in a single year is no small feat. Of the 1,500 people who are expected to attempt such a trek in 1997, the vast majority of them (about 80%) will wind up cutting their trips short for any number of reasons, including injuries, weariness, lack of time and/or money, discouragement, and just plain lack of trail sense.

While there is no definitive starting time or date for northbound thru-hikers, the general rule of thumb is to begin hiking in late March or early April and keep on going until late summer or early fall (September/October), by which time everyone should have reached Baxter State Park and Mount Katahdin, the spectacular northern terminus of the AT.

This area of the White Mountains has seen its share of residents successfully tackle the trail in recent years. To name just a few locals who've ventured the length of the AT in an end-to-end hike, there's Sue Labrie-Kenn and her dad, Meredith "Ted" Bartlett of Lincoln,

Brian DeGrace, also of Lincoln, and Ollie LaFlamme and Carol Hemenway of Littleton. Others, like Bob Every and his sons of Easton, hiked the AT over a period of years. And there are still others who are nearing a full sweep of the AT, but who also need to finish off a trail segment here or there to become officially certified AT thruhikers.

A lot of people over the years have asked me whether I've ever contemplated a thru-hike of the AT. I guess it's only natural for them to assume that I'd be interested in such a trek, since it's obvious by the very existence of this column that I am passionate about hiking and mountain climbing. But I always surprise these questioners by responding with a resounding "No!" for an answer.

Certainly a thru-hike of the AT is an enticing proposition for anyone who professes to love the sport of hiking, and I definitely fall into that particular category. Still, a thru-hike isn't and shouldn't be the "be all" or "end all" for every tramper. And I'm living proof of that.

There are lots of reasons why I'll never set foot on Springer Mountain in March or April. It is for these same reasons, of course, that you'll probably never catch me tramping along the ridge crest of South Mountain in Maryland in June, or find me lugging a 40- or 50-pound pack across Kittatinny Ridge in northern New Jersey in the brutal heat of July.

For starters, I am ashamedly a creature of comfort. Despite my avowed love for the outdoors and the immense enjoyment I've received from my backpacking ventures in the White, Green and Adirondack Mountains of the Northeast, five or six days away from my own bed is about all my frail body has ever been willing to take. I have never gotten used to sleeping on foreign soil for any great length of time, and generally speaking, after three or four sleepless nights out on the trail, I am usually in a zombie-like state of mind, with my brain focussed solely on a posturepedic mattress, a warm shower, and 24 full hours of uninterrupted sleep.

My brain, I have learned, immediately dismisses any notion of an extended backpacking trip. It sends signals to all parts of my body, telling them to rebel against this outlandish proposition. My back suddenly gets achy, my heels start to blister, and lameness promptly sets in whenever the words "Appalachian Trail" are even mentioned in passing.

Physically, I'm also in no shape to walk 2,160 miles, or whatever the AT mileage figure is nowadays. I'm especially in no shape to walk that distance lugging all my daily living trail necessities on my back. Truth is, I've never gotten used to shouldering a backpack for even a four- or five-day backwoods expedition.

Some of my worst trail experiences have taken place with a loaded pack weighting me down. The last time I set off into the woods for a two-night trip along Vermont's Long Trail (on a segment that is a link in the AT), I thought my body was going to give out on me after just a day and half of walking. I suppose part of my problem stems from carrying too much unnecessary gear in my pack. AT thru-hikers learn quickly the difference between what's nice to have in the backpack and what's absolutely necessary. The "nice to have" stuff gets sent home early on in the trip. After that it's the bare essentials and nothing else. I'm not sure I could survive on the trail for any great length of time without a couple extra pairs of pants, my personal stereo system (i.e. Walkman), or my oversized binoculars, my weighty 35mm camera, and a pound package of red licorice.

There are also, of course, all the woodland creatures who'd be my neighbors and companions for the better part of six months. Now I could deal with seeing an occasional moose or deer on the trail. But the thought of running into a pack of wild boars, or engaging in a close encounter with a rattlesnake or an ornery black bear (both of which are real possibilities on the AT) tends to raise the hair on my neck and send chills through my aforementioned achy spine. The real scourge of the backcountry, though, are the mice, who I suspect permanently inhabit every shelter, cabin or lean-to between Springer Mountain and Katahdin. I have long had a fear and contempt for this dastardly little species. Mice have already kept me awake too many times in the past as I've tried to settle in for a night of sleep after a rugged day on the trail. It's amazing how much noise these little critters can make while foraging for scraps of food. They've also been known to ruin more than one thru-hiker's pack with their nighttime nibbling at some small cache of food tucked in an unsecured side pocket.

Mice, in fact, are one of the reasons I've always carried a Walkman radio with me on my backpack trips. Rather than lie awake on my sleep pad, listening to some mouse make his predictable evening rounds, I prefer to fall asleep with my headset attached to my ears, with the strains of music from some oldies radio station or the voice of a Red Sox play-by-play broadcaster drowning out the incessant nibbling and rustling of the mousey explorer.

One final reason for me to forego a five-month trail adventure is the unimaginable thought of spending that much time away from family and friends. Unlike many thru-hikers who take to the trail to get away from the so-called "real world," I've no interest or compelling reason to leave behind the rest of civilization as I know it. I suspect that if I had to live out of a backpack for five months, I could learn to live with repetitious meals of pasta or rice, and the soggy days of early spring and humid conditions of midsummer. But there are some things in life I'd never get used to, or even want trying to get used to; one of them being staying away from my loving wife for such a dreadfully long stretch.

I live a good, not a great life here in the White Mountains. There will always be room for improvement. But taking off on an Appalachian Trail hike wouldn't make life better for me. Not now. Not before. I think I'll continue to spend my springs in New Hampshire, and leave the serious hiking (and the mice) to someone else.

One Man's Hiking Favorites

July 19, 1995

Most every hiker or backwoods explorer of the White Mountains has that one favorite place he or she likes to visit time and time again, year after year after year.

For some, it may be mean a particular mountaintop from which the tramper can gaze into the valley far below or perhaps toward the many other peaks which dot the northern New England landscape. For others it may mean some secluded pond nestled under the craggy cliffs of a nameless ridgeline.

In truth, it could be anywhere in these hills and mountains of New Hampshire. The choices are numerous, the possibilities almost endless.

As I hike around these White Mountains and talk with people on the trails, the enduring questions I am always asked are: What's your favorite mountain? What are the toughest mountains to climb? What peak has the best view?

I try to answer these queries as best I can, but often it is difficult. That's because I find it hard to choose one viewpoint or mountain-top or trail over another.

Certainly from a view standpoint, every mountain offers something different, something unique. No two summits offer exactly the same point of view, and many are equally splendid.

Trail difficulty is also tough to gauge as so much depends on the prevailing weather conditions and the "state of mind" of a hiker. I know I have experienced some of my toughest trail days on mountains that normally are not considered hard to climb, yet I have breezed my way up some of the region's most strenuous footpaths.

Although it is no easy task—for the reasons just mentioned—I will bow to public pressure just this once and compile a list or two of some of what I think are the White Mountains' most special places. Bear in mind, however, I may change my thinking on these list rankings as soon as tomorrow, or next week. Then again, maybe they'll never change.

Favorite 4,000-Footers

1. MOUNT BONDCLIFF Although there are several high peaks with better views than this 4,265-foot peak overlooking the heart of the Pemigewasset Wilderness, none evokes in me the feeling and sentiment that this mountain does. The fact that it was the handpicked last 4,000-footer I climbed back when I finished off the peakbagging list eight years ago certainly has something to do with its No. 1 ranking. Its great view and sheer cliffs and ledges also weigh heavily in my consideration.

2. MOUNT GARFIELD The summit view down into the northwest reaches of the Pemi Wilderness stands out in my mind as one of the most captivating in all the Whites. I can sit for hours on this summit (and usually do) and never tire of its magnificence.

3. MOUNT CARRIGAIN A 19th-century writer called this peak the "Watchtower of the Wilderness." It's a long five-mile haul into this mountain, but every step of the way is worth it once you're standing atop the summit viewing tower.

4. MOUNT HANCOCK The last of the great unexplored 4,000-footers, a hike up the twin peaks of this mountain evokes memories of years gone by when it took two days of strenuous tramping to reach its then trailless top.

5. NORTH TWIN It's on my list for one reason, and one reason only. I love the view south and west toward South Twin, AMC's Galehead Hut, Mount Garfield, and the peaks of the Franconia Range. It's among the best in my book.

Least Favorite 4,000-footers

1. OWL'S HEAD Can you believe people hike nine miles (one-way) to the summit of this mountain and then get no view at the top? The hike out always feels even longer. Why bother, you ask? Because it's on The List, that's why.

Hikers carefully make their way along the rocks aside picturesque Thoreau Falls in the Pemigewasset Wilderness.

2–5. SAME AS NO. 1   That's how much I despise this mountain.

Favorite Trails

1. ZEALAND TRAIL   This path into the heart of the once fire-scarred Zealand Valley can be enjoyed by hikers young and old alike. It's got just about everything one could ask for in a trail, except steep grades. Streams, beaver ponds, moose, and mountain views all complement this footpath. Knowing the history of the Zealand Valley just adds to the allure of a hike on this trail.

2. FRANCONIA RIDGE TRAIL   The walk across the open ridge-line from Mount Lafayette to Little Haystack Mountain is among the finest in the northeast. Perhaps only the walk across Mount Katahdin's "Knife Edge" is any finer.

3. THOREAU FALLS TRAIL   It's remote and uncrowded, and in the fall of the year, is stunning, especially as one walks alongside the North Fork as its drains out of Ethan Pond.

4. EDMANDS PATH   This is perhaps the least demanding approach trail onto the Presidential Range. As I effortlessly make

Hidden Ammonoosuc Lake in the Crawford Notch region is among the finest lazy day destinations in the White Mountains

my way up to Mount Eisenhower along this graded, moderate trail, I always marvel at the work of its builder, pioneer trail-maker J. Rayner Edmands, who relocated and reconstructed this namesake path in 1909.

5. MOUNT TRIPYRAMID TRAIL   Ascending the steep slide on the North Peak and descending the rocky, gravelly slide on the South Peak makes for a rugged but unique hike along this trail. If you're just starting out in the sport of hiking, wait a few years before you try this trail out for size. It's a tough one.

Best Lazy Day Destinations

1. AMMONOOSUC LAKE   This hidden gem near Crawford Notch is perfect for a day when the legs don't want to climb but the heart says get out and hike. The mile-long loop hike around the pond (beginning at the AMC's Crawford Notch Hostel) is ideal for young hikers.

2. BALD MOUNTAIN   For the 15 minutes is takes to get from the base of Cannon Mountain Ski Area to the summit of this 2,340-foot peak, you can't beat what you get. Always a great lunch

spot, and even better towards dusk as the sun sets behind the Green Mountains of Vermont well to the west.

3. Georgianna Falls   Another little gem that thankfully sees less foot traffic than either of the two previously mentioned trails. The half-mile walk to the lower falls is easy, and the flat rocks at the base of the falls are ideal for a mid-afternoon snooze.

4. Trestle Trail   Branching off the popular Sugarloaf Trail in Twin Mountain, this short footpath follows along the Zealand River, then crosses it via a recently rebuilt wooden bridge. Can you find the old railroad grade this trail now partially utilizes?

5. North Twin Trail   Just the first mile or mile and a half on this trail satisfies me on a hot, steamy summer day. Get to the first crossing of the Little River, sit on a conveniently placed boulder resting in the middle of the stream. Take off your hiking boots and socks, and cool yourself off by dipping your toes into the icy cold waters of the mountain stream. That's how you really spell R-E-L-I-E-F.

The Four Seasons

Spring Hiker's Diary

On this early spring day, the skies are clear and the temperature is soaring into the upper 60s. It's too nice to be cooped up in the office, so I take an extended lunch break and opt to explore the woodlands alongside Mann's Hill Road in Littleton.

During the previous winter I had undertaken a couple of ventures along the base of Mount Parker, and once even made it to what I assumed was the summit. There is no real pronounced high point on the mountain, which extends north out of Littleton proper and towards Dalton.

My objective for this day is to figure out the best route to the summit area, and this proves tougher than expected as the woods are crisscrossed with a series of ATV trails and old logging roads. I eventually make it to the summit, but only after a warm and exhausting bushwhack up the east slope of the mountain. There are only a few traces of snow to be found on the wooded mountaintop, but plenty of mud.

My only view of the day is gained when I bushwhack out to a partially hidden ledge due east of the main summit. From this spot I see before me the main ridges of the White Mountains; from Kinsman Ridge in Franconia Notch, north all the way to Mount Starr King and Waumbek in Jefferson.

What a spot to be in when you're trying to hide from your boss.

MAY 4, 1991   It's been a trying month for me as two springtime injuries have kept me off the beaten path for several weeks. A broken toe sidelined me for 10 days. Then at work one day a few weeks back

I accidentally stabbed my hand with a knife. The resulting nerve damage required that I wear a cast on my right arm for a week.

Feeling the need to get out into the woods, I venture down to the Ellsworth area for an overnight backpacking trip to what is known as the Three Ponds area. It's a painless two-mile trip to the middle pond, the largest of the three. Even with a heavy pack, I am there in just an hour's walking time.

At the Three Ponds Shelter I run into three fishermen who had camped here the night before. They tell me that stormy weather the previous evening kept them awake most of the night. Winds gusted up to 50 miles an hour, and were accompanied at times by a drenching rain.

I pitch my one-man tent on a little knoll at the north end of the middle pond. There's still just enough of a breeze to force me to don a sweater as I prepare for an evening campfire and a meal.

My dinner plans go awry when my camping stove decides it doesn't want to work. I manage to boil one pot of water over the campfire, which I'll use to make instant soup. What I don't notice, of course, is that the plastic mug I've brought along with me has a crack in it, so when I pour the water into the cup, the soup leaks out and dinner is ended with barely a spoonful winding up in my hungry mouth.

You can tell it must be the first camping trip of the season.

MAY 11, 1991   It's always nice to get that first high peak of the season under one's belt, and what better way to the start the hiking year than climbing to Mount Garfield's bare summit.

This 4,500-foot mountain has always been among my favorites. Its view into the Pemigewasset Wilderness—particularly into the 13 Falls area at the north end of massive Owl's Head Mountain—is superb. The same can be said for the view toward Mount Lafayette and the high peaks of nearby Franconia Ridge.

This is springtime hiking at its best. It's pleasantly warm (65 degrees at the summit), black fly season is still a week or two away, and with the exception of a few trail maintenance workers, there's hardly anyone else in the woods today.

I'm not surprised when I run into ice and snow near the summit. The protected north slope of the mountain has yet to lose its winter coating of white, and the final quarter-mile climb to the summit, up the steep, icy footway, is tricky in places.

My summit stay is a prolonged one. It includes a 30-minute nap, lunch, a few tunes on the Walkman, and a lengthy conversation with a fellow hiker planning to spend the evening at Garfield shelter, a half-mile below the summit. By the time I sling my pack on my back for the five-mile trip down off the mountain, I have been on the summit for better than three hours.

Certainly those were the shortest three hours I've had all year.

MAY 16–19, 1991   If it's May, it must be time for my annual out-of-state hiking trip, and this year's adventure takes me and two companions to the coast of Maine and scenic Mount Desert Island and Acadia National Park.

Having never been much of an ocean buff, I'm not sure what to expect during our planned four-day visit. But it doesn't take me long to decide that this is one beautiful place to be, with its unusual mixture of rugged mountains and the open sea.

Every day of our stay takes us to a different mountaintop. We climb Mount Pemetic (1,248 feet) late on Thursday, then scale the precipitous walls of The Beehive (520 feet), Mount Penobscot (1,194 feet) and Sargent Mountain (1,373 feet) on Friday and Saturday.

Although the mountains here are low, at least from an elevation standpoint, they are a true challenge. Iron rungs attached to the rocks are needed to climb certain portions of the trails. From the summits, far-reaching views dazzle the eye. We marvel at the sights, which include the Atlantic Ocean, the rocky Maine coastline, and the interior of Maine, including the far off summit of Mount Katahdin, the state's tallest mountain.

Though we never actually hike to Mount Desert's highest peak—1,530-foot Mount Cadillac—we do manage to drive up to its summit twice. On Saturday, the nicest day of the long weekend, we view a marvelous sunset from up there. We are joined by perhaps a dozen other summit visitors, plus a curious red fox that wanders out of the woods near our car to check out who's tramping around on its home turf.

JUNE 9, 1991   It's hard to believe it's been more than three years since I last climbed to the top of the northeast's highest mountain, but it's true. Mount Washington's busy summit has kept me away in recent years, but now is as good a time as any to get reacquainted with the infamous Rock Pile.

As I usually do, I attack the mountain from the west, ascending via the Ammonoosuc Ravine Trail and the Cog Railway base area. I reach the Appalachian Mountain Club's Lakes of the Clouds hut in less than two hours, but don't stop there, not even for a five minute break. Instead I charge on up to the summit of 5,385-foot Mount Monroe, the sharp, rocky peak towering high above the hut and alpine lakes to the south.

Oddly, all the hikers I have seen (and passed) during the walk up the Ammonoosuc Ravine Trail have chosen to head directly to Mount Washington and have bypassed the half-mile walk to Mount Monroe. That leaves me with the summit all to myself for a good 30–40 minutes. An early lunch and a change of clothes recharges my hiking batteries and soon I too am on my way up Washington's summit cone as I walk along the historic Crawford Path.

When I began the day, I had hoped to reach the summit by 1:30 p.m., so when I find out at the top that's it's not even 1 o'clock yet, I am delighted with my quick progress. As expected, the summit is crowded with train passengers and families who have driven to the top of the mountain via the Auto Road. I escape the crowds for a while by ducking into the Mount Washington Observatory Museum with one of its employees, whom I became friends with a few years back when we both worked at the Mount Washington Hotel.

By 2:15 I am ready to begin my descent, and I make sure I have time to take a little side trip to the rim of the Great Gulf to try and spot a twin engine plane that crashed there last fall, killing several people. In a gully, several hundred feet below the top of the rim, I spot the scattered wreckage that still litters the wall of the great glacially-carved ravine. I am tempted to make my way down to the plane, but decide against it. It is not going anywhere, I tell myself. Maybe next time I come up here I'll investigate further, though who knows when that next time will be.

Summer Hiker's Diary

June 16, 1996

Black flies are the bane of all who have outdoor work to do in the early days of summer. No matter how you're dressed, or how well you've covered your body (either with clothing or bug dope), the little suckers always find a way to get at you.

For years, my hiking solution in June has been to head into New Hampshire's true high country—the Presidential Range—where one is almost always apt to find enough wind blowing above treeline to keep the bugs at bay.

On this pleasant, sunny June Sunday, dozens of other trampers have followed my lead and are making their way along the Crawford Path to the peaks of the Southern Presidentials. Some, like myself, are headed for Mount Pierce; others have opted to venture a bit further north to Pierce's neighbor, 4,761-foot Mount Eisenhower, the 11th highest peak in the state.

After hearing reports just a week or so earlier that snow can still be found in protected pockets in the higher elevations, I find none of the lingering white stuff, not even at 4,310 feet above sea level—or the summit elevation. Instead, I find a small platoon of hikers, and hordes of black flies taking advantage of a rare windless day along the ridge to feast on some human flesh and blood.

How bad are the black flies? Bad enough that I'm forced to don long pants—even in the mild 65 degree temperatures—just to keep them from nibbling away at my exposed legs.

My summit stay is limited to 45 minutes—there is only so much one can take—even though the weather is ideal for early summer hiking. As I loop around to AMC's Mizpah Spring Hut, less than a mile from Pierce's summit, I gratefully secure a spot inside the building where I can eat my lunch in peace and not share a single bite with the bloodthirsty black flies.

JULY 24, 1996   In my many travels up and down the mountains of New Hampshire, I have somehow missed taking the trail that climbs to the top of Mount Tecumseh (near Waterville Valley) from the north.

In four previous hikes to Tecumseh's 4,004-foot summit, I have always taken the east branch of the Mount Tecumseh Trail to get to the pointy mountaintop. In years past, this meant walking a ways along the not-so-wilderness-like ski trails of Waterville Valley. This time I have decided on a different summit approach.

Joined by two elderly gents from the Landaff area, the three of us begin our day's adventure from the height-of-land on Tripoli Road and begin the mild ascent of Tecumseh along an old logging road.

Our first objective on this trip will be Tecumseh's west peak, a mountain that was formerly listed on one New England peakbagging list, but was dropped when a resurvey of the mountain revealed it was either smaller than once believed, or there wasn't a large enough rise from the col between it and Tecumseh's main peak to continue qualifying for the list.

We are surprised the grade is so easy and we are atop the mostly viewless west peak in just a couple of easy hours of walking. Next it's on to Tecumseh's main summit, which while not the most exciting in the Whites, is certainly much visited by those staying in the nearby Valley.

After an extended lunch and much conversation with fellow hikers at the top, we decide to stroll a ways over toward the top of the ski area, where several viewpoints along the ridge were cut a few years back. These views—one facing northwest, the other east—provide the best panoramas of the day.

On the way to the views, I suffer a pretty nasty gash on my left shin when I smack my leg on a protruding rock. It smarts some, but hopefully not enough to be noticeable. We hikers are supposed to be a tough lot. A little blood shed in the face of a rocky ascent is as much a medal of honor as anything. I'll wear the wound proudly for the rest of the summer.

AUGUST 17, 1996   Nothing grand planned for today. I've offered to lead a hike for the North Country YMCA Outing Club up to scenic Arethusa Falls in Crawford Notch. It's not my first choice of places to visit on a busy midsummer weekend, but that's not the point on this day. I'm here to introduce a few downcountry folk to the beauty of the White Mountains.

The southern New Hampshire hikers joining me for the trek are middle-aged, ambitious, but admittedly out of shape. The slow, steady pace I set along the rough and tumble trail to the falls proves a bit much for the couple at times. As there's no great rush to get to the falls, I won't complain.

The 45-minute stroll brings back memories of my last trip on this trail just over a year ago, when a Massachusetts hiker was killed in a fall from atop the 200-foot high falls. On that day I was covering the event as a reporter for a local newspaper, and the scene was a grim one as rescuers struggled to carry the lifeless body of the hiker out to a waiting hearse.

Although the large crowd of hikers at the falls is enjoying this day, I'm a little more subdued than normal. The 1995 tragedy at Arethusa Falls lingers in my head. This is just too beautiful a spot for something of that nature to occur.

SEPTEMBER 19, 1996   My annual mid-September vacation hasn't lived up to its billing so far this week. Rainy days and cloudy mountaintops have predominated over the first five days. Today I'm hoping to finally see the sun.

It's cool and windy as I strike off from the base of Cannon Mountain and begin the steep ascent to the top of the famed Old Man of the Mountain.

Utilizing a nontechnical rock climber's route—an unmaintained, unblazed path along Cannon's north-facing slopes—I quickly warm up to the task by pulling and pushing my way up and up and up towards the Old Man. By 8:30 I have reached the same elevation as Eagle Pass, a mile or so away across Franconia Notch. As I step out of the sheltered woods and onto the exposed rocks which form the great rock profile, I am blasted by a gust of wind that nearly whisks my baseball cap off my head and down over the Old Man's forehead.

Alone with the Old Man for the next 90 minutes, I strike up a one-sided conservation with the old gent and relate how jealous I am of the grand vista he has before him each and every day. Profile Lake, some 1,200 feet below, sparkles green as the sun glances down on its waters after rising above the towering Franconia Ridge peaks to the east.

Peering out and down over the ledges which form the top of the Old Man, I marvel at the courage (or foolhardiness) of the rock climbers who dare scale the sheer face of the Cannon Cliffs; their lives entrusted to a rope and pins hammered into the rock walls.

By 10 a.m. I am ready to bid the Old Man and another summer season a fond farewell.

It's been great getting to know you both. I just wish summer would hang around as long as the Great Stone Face.

Winter Hiker's Diary

Who's kidding whom here? The calendar shows it's not winter yet, but you'll have a hard time convincing me otherwise.

On the hiking itinerary this morning is Mount Garfield, the pyramid-shaped peak nestled halfway between the Franconias and Mount Lafayette to the west and the wild and rugged Twin Range to the east.

The temperature is frigid, as it has been since the start of the month, and yesterday's heavy snowfall has blanketed the trees with a fresh coat of white powder. The overcast skies portend additional snow flurries throughout the day. Undoubtedly, some time during our planned 12-mile trek, we'll be walking among the falling snowflakes.

With more than a dozen hikers on this AMC-sponsored trip, we take turns breaking trail as we zigzag our way across the northern slopes of the mountain. We are surprised to see that someone yesterday made it nearly two-thirds of the way to the summit before retreating. Why anyone would have attempted this hike in Saturday's blizzard is beyond me.

It takes us five hours to reach the concrete remains of the old fire lookout at the summit. The wind is fierce at the top, and the clouded sky allows no views on this day.

I take out my camera for a summit shot or two, but the zero degree temperature has sapped all the power from my camera's battery. I manage to get off one shot before the battery goes completely dead. Meanwhile my exposed fingers nearly freeze in the process.

Five minutes after reaching the summit the entire group is headed back down the trail, unable to withstand any longer the bitter cold of the summit. Several in our group already are showing early signs of frost nip, including Creston Ruiter of Whitefield, who's out on his first ever winter snowshoe hike. A quick retreat is definitely in order.

By the time we reach Route 3, where our cars are parked, the skies have finally cleared but it's still mighty cold. A hot meal will taste good tonight.

JANUARY 1, 1990   It's a tradition now to start off the New Year with a mountain climb. Last year my hiking friend Steve Smith and I plodded our way up Mount Jackson. This year Steve, Creston and I are back in the Crawford Notch area again, this time aiming for the summit of Mount Tom.

When we start off at the Crawford railroad depot, we have our snowshoes hitched to our packs, figuring the chosen ascent route up the Avalon and A–Z Trails has been packed out this past week by holiday vacationers. Less than 100 yards into the hike, it's obvious we're dead wrong. On go the snowshoes and up goes the trail.

The weather forecasters are calling for a decent hiking day, but a mile or so into our walk, a heavy snow squall strikes. The falling snow, combined with a brisk, southerly breeze, makes for a chillier than expected day on the trail.

After leaving the Avalon Trail 1.4 miles from Route 302 and the Notch, the trail grade steepens and Creston, hiking in newly purchased snowshoes, has a tough time keeping up with Steve and me.

Within a couple of hours we hit the top of the ridge and bear right onto the Mount Tom Spur. Along this trail we encounter a number of blowdowns, which force us at one point to crawl on our hands and knees as we attempt to pass under them.

The wooded summit of Mount Tom is unattractive and uninviting, though limited views are available from several points away from the top of the peak. Occasionally we are able to catch a glimpse southward to neighboring Mount Field and westward to the back side of Whitewall Mountain near Zealand Notch.

During our descent, as we slab across the headwall of the great basin separating Mount Tom from Mount Field, a strong gust of wind creates whiteout conditions along the trail. Visibility is no more than six or seven feet. It is easy to see, under conditions like this, how winter Presidential Range hikers frequently get turned around when caught in a snowstorm while above the treeline.

JANUARY 14, 1990   My second winter peakbagging journey of the season finds Steve, Creston and me in Gorham. Our objective is 4,047-foot Mount Moriah.

For a change, the skies are clear, but it is fiercely cold. This will be my coldest winter hike ever.

The long, strenuous climb via the Carter–Moriah Trail would be a lot easier if it were tracked out properly for snowshoeing. What has happened, though, is that someone has recently barebooted their way up the trail, leaving boot tracks (or postholes) 12 inches deep along the way. The boot tracks just aren't conducive to good snowshoeing, so the going proves slower than usual.

Clad in our matching pairs of Sherpa snowshoes, we make our way slowly skyward. Open ledges on Mount Surprise treat us to splendid views of the northern Presidentials and Mount Washington. We can even see wisps of blowing snow near Washington's summit, certain evidence the mountaintop will be extra cold today.

Despite an abundance of sunshine, the thermometer on my backpack never rises about five degrees all day. On the summit at 1 p.m. it reads one degree below zero. Thirty minutes later the temperature is six degrees lower.

By successfully reaching Moriah, I have now bagged 45 of the 48 Four Thousand Footers of New Hampshire in winter. I am sure I'll complete the list before winter's end, but with three tough mountains (Jefferson, Owl's Head and Zealand) still to go, I know it won't be easy.

JANUARY 21, 1990   No big summits today. Just a little winter bushwhacking instead. Franconia Notch's Eagle Cliff, admired by many but climbed by few, is where we hope to end up. Whether we make it or not will depend on the off-trail snow conditions and the navigability of the short but rugged ridge which branches out from Eagle Cliff's summit to the northwest.

The first little knob along the ridge proves easier to reach than we expect as we stumble across what appears to be the remnants of an old, flagged route up the mountainside. At one time in the mid-1960s the state was considering a trail across this entire ridge. We wonder if this is what remains of that effort.

A short and steep climb gets us quickly to the open summit of this knob, but because it is snowing in the Notch, we get no views. We can hear skiers across the way at Cannon Mountain, but can't see them. We get the voices, but no picture. A strange scenario indeed.

For the most part the woods along the lower heights of the ridge are open and easy to poke around in, but as we go further along the crest of the ridge, and near its highest points, the forest thickens into a tangle of windblown trees.

It takes us nearly four hours to traverse barely two miles, but we finally attain Eagle Cliff's wooded summit at 2 p.m. Since this is a peak on the New Hampshire Three Thousand Footer list, there is a small register sheet for us to add our names to. A quick review of the enclosed entries reveals we are the first to reach the summit since mid-October and are only the second group of hikers to get there in winter in the last six years.

We earned this summit, that's for sure. No wonder it doesn't have many winter friends.

A Preference for Autumn

September 23, 1994

The sweltering heat of summer has passed us by now. The oppressive humidity and visibility-reducing haze of July and August have concluded their annual North Country visit.

For hikers, the departure of summer and the onset of autumn ushers in more than a new calendar season. It is the time of year when the changing colors of the forest canopy illuminate the backwoods trails. It is the time of year when the peaks and valleys of the White Mountains are most inviting.

Most hikers, myself included, prefer this time of year over any other. The cooler days of September and early October are a refreshing treat from the sticky, discomforting 90 degree days of midsummer. Far-reaching views, so infrequent during the hazy days of summer, are the rule rather than the exception on most early autumn days.

There are other pluses as well for the fall hiker. Foot traffic, for instance, is negligible during midweek as many of last month's hikers are either back in school or have used up their allotted vacation time. And for the hiker with the sweet tooth (and the pack full of chocolate candy bars), the crisper fall air extends the pack life of one's Hershey bars and M&M's—both of which are often melting messes by the time one stops to indulge during a July hike.

Fall hiking has its down side as well, unfortunately. Early morning trampers can expect to be greeted with near-freezing temperatures as they strike off for their destinations. For backpackers, especially those camping in the higher elevations, the nighttime air can be downright cold and raw, especially on a cloudy or wet night. Likewise, a trip onto the Presidential Range or to majestic Mount Lafayette high above Franconia Notch can mean a brush with early snowfall, or at minimum, ice-coated footpaths and stream beds.

As the season progresses, one's pack must also become proportionately more crowded. An extra tee shirt and perhaps a light jacket are no longer sufficient to shield one from the elements. Winter hats and gloves are jammed alongside one's wind pants, wool sweater and water bottle. Thermos jugs of hot chocolate or warm apple cider have replaced the refreshingly cool bottles of soda pop and lemonade.

An autumn hiker's toughest decision can often be choosing where he or she will visit. Will it be a peak like 4,802-foot Mount Moosilauke, with its extensive views westward toward Vermont's Green Mountain's and New York's distant Adirondacks, or will it be into the peaceful Zealand Valley, where J. E. Henry's logging locomotives once routinely visited?

No matter the chosen destination, it's a "no lose" situation for a tramper.

If you're heading out into the woods over the coming weeks, and haven't yet figured out where to go, consult the Appalachian Mountain Club's *AMC White Mountain Guide* or one of the many other fine guidebooks available throughout the region in bookstores and other retail outlets. As for my recommendations, well, I don't even know where to begin. But here are a few choice spots I've been known to visit during the autumn foliage hiking season:

THOREAU FALLS   The fact that this picturesque waterfall (named after 19th-century writer and naturalist Henry David Thoreau) is five miles distant from the nearest roadway should not discourage hikers of any age from paying a visit to this scenic and remote spot. The trek to Thoreau Falls generally follows old railroad grades, thus the terrain is gentle and the footing quite adequate. To reach Thoreau Falls one must first pass through Zealand Valley and the nearby Zealand Falls Hut (operated by AMC). The walk through rocky Zealand Notch remains one of the mountain region's most rewarding tramps. The falls themselves, on the North Fork of the Pemigewasset River, are particularly spectacular after a rainstorm. But even in dry weather they are worth a visit for the view from the granite slabs at the top of the falls offer a unique perspective of the vast Pemi Wilderness below and to the south and west.

MOUNT MOOSILAUKE   There are a handful of ways to reach the summit of this 4,802-foot mountain—the easternmost 4,000-footer in the Whites. Many hikers prefer to climb from the Dartmouth Outing Club's Ravine Lodge in Woodstock at the southeast base of the peak. Others prefer the steep but scenic ascent along the Beaver Brook Trail out of Kinsman Notch (Route 112). Perhaps the least used, but easiest ascent route is via the Benton Trail off Tunnel Brook Road. It's 3.6 moderate hiking miles from the trailhead to the summit, and the final two-tenths of a mile are along Moosilauke's exposed, flat summit ridgeline. Although this mountain has few close neighbors, the view from its summit is superb. Not only are a majority of the White Mountains' highest peaks seen, but also most of Vermont's tallest mountains and the nearby winding Connecticut River Valley.

MOUNT JACKSON   For the aspiring peakbagger, a venture to the top of this 4,052-foot mountain in the Southern Presidentials is a challenging, but nonthreatening test.

The 2.6-mile hike to Jackson's open summit is tough enough to make one work up a sweat, but short enough to enable even the out-of-shape tramper to make it all the way to the top. Because only the immediate summit area is open and exposed to the elements, little of the inherent dangers that too often strike down hikers on the Presidentials are present on this mountain.

The trail starts at the top of Crawford Notch on the north side of Route 302 (the Webster-Jackson Trail). Side paths to prominent Elephant's Head and Bugle Cliff offer trampers valid excuses to take breaks from their climbing chores.

From Jackson's summit, the peaks of the Southern Presidentials dominate the view to the northeast. To the south and west lies massive Mount Willey. To the north and west are the peaks of the Twin Range, plus 4,054-foot Mount Hale—another mountain that aspiring peakbaggers often take on early in their quest to climb all of New Hampshire's 4,000-foot summits.

The classic view of Crawford Notch as seen from the summit of Mount Willard.

Mount Willard　　If you don't mind the massive weekend crowds that flock to this longtime favorite overlooking Crawford Notch, the walk to this 2,850-foot peak remains one of the White Mountains region's best family hikes.

With the exception of a short, moderately strenuous stretch of trail about a half a mile into the hike, the terrain is gentle and the walking easy, thus hikers of all ages find this trail to their liking.

As the *AMC White Mountain Guide* has long professed, there are few hikes in the region that "afford so grand a view . . . for so little effort." The sweeping view from the summit ledges encompasses the floor of the Notch, the Conway Scenic Railroad grade, towering Mounts Willey and Webster on each side of the Notch, and distant views southward toward Mount Chocorua.

My Rules
on Winter Hiking

January 4, 1996

In case you hadn't noticed, winter is here in all its splendor and glory, and snowshoers and hikers are once again taking to the snow-covered woods.

Winter hiking is a sport unto itself. It has its own rules, its own passionate followers. It's completely different from spring, summer and fall hiking.

Over the years there have been plenty of books written about winter hiking. A few that quickly come to mind are John Danielsen's *Winter Hiking and Camping* published by the Adirondack Mountain Club, Garrett and Alexandra Conover's *A Snow Walker's Companion*, and Stephen Gorman's *AMC Guide to Winter Camping*.

While I don't profess to have as much knowledge about winter camping or backpacking as the above mentioned authors do, I've been around enough in the woods to know what makes for a successful, enjoyable day hike this time of year.

I present to you, therefore, my five basic rules or guidelines for winter hiking.

1. *Always figure your winter hike is going to take longer than your original estimate.*

If you've ever done any tramping around in the winter woods, whether on the trail or off, you already know that the going can be tedious, exhausting, and sometimes next to impossible. When you add in the difficulty of climbing upwards maybe 3,500 to 4,000 feet, that makes matters even tougher.

When estimating times of ascent, you can almost automatically throw out the times listed in hiking guides. Certainly if the trail you've chosen has yet to be broken out by previous snowshoers, the ascent will be that much more difficult and that much more time-consuming.

Much, of course, will depend on the size of the group you're hiking with, the physical condition of group members, and trail conditions. Nothing slows a winter hike down more than frequent rest stops by weaker group members. Obviously icy trail conditions, or wet, heavy, unbroken snow are also roadblocks.

2. *The more hikers in your group, the merrier it will be.*

While one of the biggest attractions of winter hiking is the fact that the woods are uncrowded and the opportunities for solitude are greatly enhanced, a solo snowshoe hike up a mountain after a two-foot dumping of snow just isn't much fun.

Ideally, your winter hiking group should number 3–5 people. This allows for a generous number of reinforcements when it comes to breaking trail, while at the same time keeping the size of the pack to a manageable number.

Having taken part in group hikes with upwards of 25 people, I can assure you that's too many bodies, too many voices, and too many headaches if you're the designated group leader. At the opposite end of the spectrum, hiking alone, while desirable by many, can be physically draining, and even dangerous, especially in the event of an unforeseen accident, such as a fall.

3. *Prepare for the worst, and hope for the best.*

There's a reason why the White Mountains, and in particular Mount Washington and the Presidential Range, have a reputation for being amongst the most inhospitable mountains in the country. The fact that well over a hundred people have died on the Presidentials, and numerous others elsewhere in the White Hills, proves that the mountains can be unforgiving.

Winter is the time of year when the mountains are the most treacherous. Blinding snowstorms, bone chilling temperatures, and arctic-like wind are commonplace in these mountains. Unless you're prepared to deal with the worst that Mother Nature can conjure up, stay home, curl up in front of the fire, and read a book.

Unless they're gluttons for punishment, or are just plain fool-hardy, most winter hikers will avoid problems with the elements

The author, clad in full winter regalia, stands atop the frosty summit of Middle Sugarloaf Mountain during a winter hike in February 1995.

by simply staying away from places they shouldn't be. Inevitably, though, most winter hikers will at some point run into a situation they didn't figure on confronting. They might lose the trail in the deep snow drifts, get caught above treeline in a sudden blinding snow squall, or break through the ice and into the water while attempting what appeared to be a harmless stream crossing.

No one should strike off into the winter woods without proper clothing, footwear, maps and compass, or emergency provisions. Carrying around a little common sense doesn't hurt either. Those who've left the latter at home have been known to pay the ultimate price.

4. *Know where you're going and how to get there.*

A few years back, a friend of mine and I struck off for Mount Washington and Presidential Range one late February morning. Our itinerary for the day first called for an ascent of Washington's closest southern neighbor, Mount Monroe, then an attack on the Rock Pile itself. We planned to hike up onto the Range via the Boott Spur Trail, strike off for Monroe, take the Crawford Path up to Washington, then descend via the Lion Head Trail to Hermit Lake Shelter and the Tuckerman Ravine Trail.

When we got to the Boott Spur Trail—a path neither of us had ever hiked—we saw it hadn't been broken out yet, so rather than tire ourselves by breaking snow all the way up the ridge, we opted to reverse our route and climb Washington first, then Monroe, and eventually descend via Boot Spur.

Being in pretty good shape at the time, we had no problem reaching Washington, and little trouble with Monroe, but by the time we got to the top of Boott Spur we were exhausted and daylight was fading fast. Being unfamiliar with the Boott Spur Trail, we initially had trouble figuring out where it left the exposed ridgeline for the forested valley below. By the time we got our bearings, the sun was sinking below the horizon, and we were suddenly faced with a two-mile tramp through the darkening woods, on a trail which we'd never traversed, and which we suspected was still not broken out.

In this instance, we lucked out as the trail had indeed been used by someone else earlier in the day. And despite the fading daylight, we were able to follow the snowshoe tracks safely through the woods and back to the Tuckerman Ravine Trail.

To this day, I am convinced we'd never have gotten out of the woods as easily as we did if not for the person or persons who'd broken out the Boott Spur Trail sometime between the time we'd passed it by earlier and the time we were ready to descend it later in the day.

As it was, we almost lost the snowshoe track several times in the nearly dark woods. Certainly without the tracked trail, we'd have been reduced to a slow plod through the woods, and very likely would have wandered off the trail at some point, and might well have spent a night out in the cold winter air.

From that day forward, we promised to stick with trails that one (or both of us) had previously passed over in our hiking careers, and that we'd allow plenty of time for both our ascents and descents.

5. *Eat, Drink, and Be Energized.*

Nothing tastes better out on the winter trail than a cup of hot apple cider or some type of similar hot substitute. It warms your innards, reenergizes your tired body, and provides a huge psychological boost.

Packing proper food and drink items for a winter hike can be difficult, since freezing cold temperatures can wreak havoc with many foods and drinks one normally takes along in the warmer times of the year.

Sandwiches are convenient to take along, while easily digestible, high-energy foods such as dried fruits, cheeses, and gorp are staples of many winter trampers. Fresh fruit, if they can be prevented from freezing, are a choice snack food. Chocolate bars, unfortunately, tend to freeze hard as a rock in the cold, thus are not recommended for winter trail consumption.

The Roots of Winter Hiking
Go Back More Than a Century

January 25, 1995

Taking to the mountain trails in winter has gained significant popularity over the past few decades, especially with hikers bent on reaching the highest summits of the White Mountains.

Winter excursions (especially to Mount Washington and the treeless peaks of the Presidential Range) expose hikers to unique challenges and hazards. As we have witnessed over the last 13 months, frigid temperatures, bountiful amounts of snow, and poor pre-trip planning have all been contributing factors in the recent spate of accidents that have claimed the lives of several climbers.

Hiking in January and February, though admittedly tougher than a midsummer stroll through the forest, need not be as hazardous to one's health as might be perceived. With the proper equipment and clothing, and the use of a little common sense, winter hiking can be just as pleasurable, if not more so, than a hike taken any other time of the year.

In this modern era of mountain climbing, we are, of course, blessed with oodles and oodles of high tech equipment and outerwear, plus miles and miles of maintained trails. Certainly the advent of lightweight aluminum snowshoes, and the creation of synthetic fibers like Gore-Tex and polar fleece has made winter climbing a safer and more comfortable undertaking.

The fact that trails have been blazed to just about every major summit in the region is also a major plus as the exhausting work of bushwhacking up a steep mountainside is not usually part of the winter hiking regimen.

Today's winter trekker certainly has a major advantage over the hikers of the late 19th century, who in attempting to reach the high peaks of the region in winter faced more formidable opposition in their quests.

It was just over a century ago that winter climbing got its start in the northeast. According to Guy and Laura Waterman's monumental history of hiking in the region, *Forest and Crag*, the first organized snowshoeing clubs in New England were formed in the 1880s, and in the ensuing years, hikers (many of them women) began seriously attempting to reach the higher summits of the White Mountains.

New Hampshire's famed Mount Washington was the first major White Mountains peak to be explored in winter. These early winter excursions to the top of a mountain notorious for its deadly winter climate preceded by 20 years or so excursions to the region's other less dangerous summits.

The formation of the Appalachian Mountain Club's Snow-Shoe Section in the late 1880s precipitated a miniature winter hiking boom. This band of merry winter recreationists is credited with reaching the summits of Mounts Osceola, Tecumseh, North and South Tripyramid, Carrigain, Tom and Giant Stairs during the 1890s. Although it cannot be proven, it is surmised that many of these were first winter ascents.

As the Watermans note in their book, the February 24, 1896 ascent of remote Mount Carrigain is especially notable as the seven-person party included one female member, a Miss M. A. Furbish. "The reader should recall the obstacles confronting women climbers of that day, from the social restraints to the physical handicap of long skirts, which must have been frightfully heavy and awkward as the hems became coated with ice and snow," reminded the Watermans. "Considering these obstacles, Furbish's participation in such a difficult first winter ascent as Carrigain is extraordinary."

As the turn of the century neared, climbers not affiliated with the AMC Snow-Shoe Section also began making their marks on the winter hiking landscape, recording ascents up Mount Moriah in Gorham, among other places.

Many of these early winter hiking parties included a substantial number of trampers. Groups of 50 or more were not uncommon on some of these excursions.

Over the ensuing decades, as more and more trails were cut to the high peaks, and hiking to New Hampshire's highest summits became a favorite pastime of trampers, it was inevitable that someone would soon take on the daunting task of climbing all of New Hampshire's 4,000-foot peaks in winter.

Just a year after the AMC's Four-Thousand Footer Club was formed, veteran world-class mountaineers Robert and Miriam Underhill of Randolph set out to peakbag all the White Mountains 4,000-footers in winter. They successfully completed the list on December 23, 1960 on the top of 5,712-foot Mount Jefferson, despite summit winds in excess of 70 miles per hour and a high temperature of just minus seven degrees. Incredibly, Robert Underhill was 71 years of age, and Miriam, 62, when they became the first persons to complete the list of peaks some 34 years ago.

As evidenced by the number of vehicles at trailheads throughout the region each weekend, it is obvious that winter hiking continues to flourish in the White Hills of New Hampshire. On any given winter weekend, organized trips to a half dozen major peaks are not uncommon. AMC members still constitute a large percentage of these winter trampers, though other groups, such as the YMCA, also regularly offer winter hiking trips.

For persons who've never partaken in a winter hike, it's advisable that they first read up on the subject and find out what kind of equipment and clothing is needed to assure a comfortable, safe and enjoyable outing. There are plenty of books out on the market, covering subjects like snowshoeing, winter hiking and winter backpacking.

AMC also regularly offers workshops for beginning snowshoers and winter climbers—for a fee, of course. The North Country YMCA Outing Club is offering a series of winter hikes this season; many geared toward the rookie snowshoer.

Mount Washington
and the Presidentials

Fall Hike Up Mount Washington Was Only the Beginning

October 16, 1996

October can be among the cruelest of months when it comes to climbing mountains here in New Hampshire. While the colors of fall enliven life in the valleys, the high summits can be life-threatening, as we've witnessed this past week on Mount Washington, where two women climbers barely escaped the peak's all-too-frequent fatal clutches.

An October visit to the high country can bring with it all kinds of surprises—both pleasant and tragic. It may bring crystal clear skies and unforgettable views. It may bring rain and wind, or fog and snow. It can also be quite unforgiving.

For many trampers, Columbus Day weekend marks the unofficial end to the hiking season. The hordes that packed the trails Saturday and Sunday, hoping to capture the last bit of color in the deep valley floors of the White Mountains, have now disappeared.

As we enter this transition stage between autumn and winter, the mountains always preview what's to come in the weeks and months ahead. The summit snows that we see today promise to creep into the valleys sooner than many of us wish. And the leafless trees high on the rising slopes clue us in on the fact that foliage season is officially over.·

For me, the passing of the Columbus Day weekend means much more than the changing of the seasons. Instead, it brings back memories from my first year of mountain hiking, in 1982, when I could count the number of peaks I'd climbed on less than two hands.

Back then I was still a novice hiker—young, enthusiastic, and naive. But the mountain bug had already begun to infect me.

I was fresh out of college and looking for new challenges, when I took on the task of hiking mountains without really knowing what I was in for. My first few hikes were near catastrophes as I stumbled my way up the trails with practically no gear to speak of; not even a cheap pair of hiking boots.

My older brother, who'd done his share of hiking in the years leading up to 1982, had unconvincingly espoused the virtues of the sport to me for several summers. But it wasn't until I reached my first 4,000-foot peak (Mount Osceola, July 22, 1982) that I realized what all the fuss was about.

Of course one thing soon led to another, and before I knew it I had taken up my brother's invitation to hike to the top of Mount Washington on Columbus Day weekend. I accepted this challenge knowing that my previous hiking forays included nothing even remotely close to the magnitude of this adventure. So as Columbus Day neared, and I frantically tried to work myself into shape by doing a couple of warm-up hikes to the Cannon Cliffs in Franconia Notch and Wheeler Mountain in Vermont, I feared the worst and hoped for the best.

As I remember, the morning of October 10 dawned brilliant, with a near cloudless sky and temperatures hovering around the freezing mark. As I departed from my Lyndonville, Vermont home with two college buddies who had also accepted the Mount Washington challenge, I worried that I didn't have the right clothes for above treeline travel, and that my pack wasn't adequate for such an ambitious hike.

When we arrived at the trailhead (at the Cog Railway base station), my first order of business was to change out of my sneakers and don some real hiking boots. They weren't mine, mind you, but a spare pair of my brother's, whose feet just happen to be about two sizes larger than mine. To make up for the difference, I put on two pairs of heavy socks, but that was marginal protection at best. At least the shoes weren't too small (and tight), which I figured would be worse.

We started our hike along the Ammonoosuc Ravine Trail, and within minutes encountered our first ice-coated rocks of the day. Though this added to my worries, I trudged on, trying fruitlessly to keep pace with my fast-moving brother and one of my college friends, who'd also done some serious hiking in the past.

The steepness of the trail leading up to Lakes of the Clouds and the Appalachian Mountain Club's high hut of the same name was all but forgotten when we reached the first ledgy outlooks along the upper reaches of the ravine. I marveled at the view, especially as I gazed off to the west toward my native Vermont and spotted for the first time the Northeast Kingdom peaks of Burke and Umpire Mountain—two mountains I had grown up with.

A side trip from the AMC hut to the sharp summit of Mount Monroe preceded our final assault on the Rock Pile. And though I didn't realize it at the time, this trail diversion seemed to drain me of much of the energy I would soon need as I worked my way up the Crawford Path to Mount Washington's bustling summit.

As is to be expected on Columbus Day weekend, especially when conditions are favorable atop the mountain, the summit center was jam packed with people. Obviously some had arrived there by train, others by motor vehicles. I have to admit I wore my backpack with pride that day as I strolled past the gift shop and into the snack bar, passing by the hordes of people who'd made it to the mountaintop by mechanical means. Reaching the summit by foot seemed so much more rewarding than a ride on the Cog or a drive up the Auto Road. Exhausted as I was, I was glad I'd hiked to the top.

Our descent via the Jewell Trail was probably what I remember most about this initial trek up Mount Washington. I was in awe of this barren, treeless landscape, and my first glimpse into the vast ravine north of the mountain—known as the Great Gulf—still stands out as one of my most memorable mountain moments anywhere, anytime, anyplace.

As we stopped for a break atop the rim of the Great Gulf, and celebrated the moment by pouring ourselves a small cup full of wine, I knew for the first time I was seriously hooked on the mountain experience.

As we continued on down the mountain, my feet started to blister and my muscles began to ache. But all the discomfort in the world didn't matter as I became intoxicated with the panorama spread in front of me. The great northern peaks of the Presidential Range stretched out to our right, their craggy summits standing high above the floor of the Great Gulf. To the left, beyond the grade of the Cog Railway, lay the peaks of the Southern Presidentials and their many grand ridgelines sloping downward toward the vast Bretton Woods plain. And far in the distant, more to the south and west, stood many of the other White Mountains summits I would soon find myself exploring.

After finally making it down off the mountain late in the afternoon, I recall that our ride back to Vermont was a subdued one as our weary bones cried out for a hot shower and a warm bed. But all the way home, I couldn't help but smile as I thought about what I'd accomplished.

In my mind, I had passed the biggest hiking test of my life. And knowing that, I now had the confidence to strike off elsewhere in these White Hills.

For me, this October 1982 hike to New Hampshire's most famed summit represented not the end of the hiking season, but a new beginning, for it was a hike that forever changed me.

The Crawford Path:
An Alluring Mountain Trail

Here we stood . . . more than four thousand feet above the sea,
confronted by an expanse so vast that no eye but an eagle's might
grasp it so thronged with upstarting peaks as to confound and
bewilder us out of all power of expression.
— SAMUEL ADAMS DRAKE, describing the view
along the Crawford Path in his 1882 book,
The Heart of the White Mountains

June 15, 1994

One hundred and seventy-five years ago, when visits to the high peaks of the White Mountains were rare, and only the hardiest of souls bothered to investigate the upper slopes of New Hampshire's most prominent mountain range, pioneer innkeepers Abel and Ethan Allen Crawford blazed one of America's first hiking trails.

Starting near the height-of-land of the great Notch of the White Mountains, the Crawfords cut a narrow swath through the thick woods all the way to the open expanse of the rocky, treeless heights of what later would become known as the southern peaks of the Presidential Range.

The trail first passed near the summit of present-day Mount Clinton, then weaved and climbed its way past Mounts Pleasant, Franklin, and Monroe. Eventually the crude footpath would also pass by two small mountain tarns (the Lakes of the Clouds), before working its way up to New Hampshire's grandest mountain of all, Mount Washington, monarch of the Great White Hills.

For more than a century and a half, this trail from the Notch to Washington's windblown summit has been known to explorers, visi-

National Park Service worker Robin Snyder, left, plays the role of Lucy Crawford and storyteller Dwight Wilder the role of a 19th-century Appalachian hiker during a 1994 ceremony designating the Crawford Path as a National Recreation Trail.

tors and trampers as the Crawford Path, and later this month, the 175-year-old trail will be formally designated a National Recreation Trail at a ceremony June 25.

According to the U.S. Forest Service, which has been responsible for the maintenance and upkeep of the Crawford Path since 1917, the ceremony will be presided over by former Appalachian Mountain Club huts manager George Hamilton, and will include a period reenactment of a turn-of-the-century Crawford Path hike.

The Crawford Path is regarded as the northeast's oldest continuously maintained hiking trail. It is also considered the first such mountain-climbing trail to be constructed solely for the benefit of visiting tourists.

In time, the trail was improved by the Crawfords so that tourists could ride horses to the summit of Mount Washington. Abel Crawford, father of Ethan, became the first person to ride horseback to the top of Mount Washington in 1840. He was 74 years old at the time.

According to historians Laura and Guy Waterman, the Crawford Path we know today was but one of two paths the Crawfords would construct to Mount Washington in the early 19th century. Just two years after cutting the eight-mile-long original Crawford Path, Ethan Crawford blazed a second trail to Washington, this one climbing to the mountain's exposed ridgeline at a point closer to Ammonoosuc Ravine.

In fact, write the Watermans in their invaluable book, *Forest and Crag*, it was the second Crawford Path which Ethan utilized more often than not when guiding visitors up to the lofty heights of Mount Washington. "Ethan used it almost exclusively and left the original path to his father," wrote the Watermans.

Early written descriptions of the Crawford Path indicate it was barely adequate for foot travel. The Watermans said it was, at first, "but a slight improvement over the old bushwhack routes" used by the Crawfords in guiding early mountain visitors to Mount Washington.

History books also reveal that for a time in the 1870s, the Crawford Path was used sparingly by trampers and the trail became somewhat overgrown and obscure. A resurgence in interest in mountain hiking—no doubt spurred in part by the formation of the Appalachian Mountain Club in 1876—assured that the trail would again

A winter hiker emerges from the woods at the Crawford Path trailhead near Crawford Notch State Park.

be used extensively as a primary route up to Mount Washington and the peaks just south of it.

The Crawford Path as we know it today follows the same basic route of its original course, though over the years it has undergone a number of relocations. Hikers walking the trail from its starting point at Crawford Notch first pass through the Gibbs Brooks Scenic Area and its stand of tall, virgin timber. Later a side trail to the AMC's Mizpah Spring Hut is passed, followed by the trail's link-up with the 2,160-mile Appalachian Trail just below the summit of Mount Clinton.

After climbing above treeline, the Crawford Path continues for more than five miles to the top of Mount Washington. The path itself does not pass over the actual summits of Eisenhower (formerly Pleasant), Franklin or Monroe, but rather skirts their high points. Various spur paths do, however, take hikers to the true summits.

After passing along the rim of Oakes Gulf, the Crawford Path descends slightly to the Lakes of the Clouds, where the AMC has another of its high mountain huts. From Lakes, it's a 1.4-mile tramp to Washington's summit.

Because the final five miles of the trail extend across the exposed ridgeline of the Presidential Range, many a tramper on the Crawford Path has been beset by foul weather as they have proceeded along its rocky way. Most have had the sense to retreat to safer ground; others have tempted the fates and forged onward.

In his narrative of 1882, Samuel Adams Drake, proceeding along the Crawford Path with two hiking companions in less-than-ideal weather conditions, described the latter stages of his group's ascent thusly:

"We were nearing the goal; so much was certain. But the violence of the gale, increasing with the greater altitude, warned us against delay. We therefore pushed on across the stony terraces extending beyond, and were at length rewarded by seeing before us the heaped-up pile of broken granite constituting the peak of Washington, and which we knew still rose a thousand feet above our heads. The sight of this towering mass, which seems formed of the debris of the Creation, is well calculated to stagger more adventurous spirits than the three weary and footsore men who stood watching the cloud-billows, silently rolling up, dashing themselves unceasingly against its foundations. We looked first at the mountain, then in each other's faces, then began the ascent."

Unquestionably, many other trampers in 175 years have marveled at the same sights alluded to by Drake, and a like number have been confronted by his hiking group's dilemma.

That is the nature of this historical mountain trail, known as the Crawford Path.

Mount Washington:
Still Taking Lives

*There is never a moment on this grand old summit in which God
does not use it for impressions upon the sensitive mind and heart.*
　　　—JULIUS WARD, 1890, speaking of Mount Washington

May 11 and 18, 1994

New Hampshire and New England's highest mountain—6,288-foot
tall Mount Washington—has done nothing in 1994 to diminish its
standing as the region's most fascinating, and deadly peak.

This giant of the White Mountains range, known worldwide for
its inhospitable weather and its challenging terrain, has shown no
mercy to those who have attempted fate on its snow-covered, icy
slopes. In a year that is barely a third over, the mountain has already
claimed the lives of three unfortunate souls. A fourth, meanwhile,
was killed on neighboring Mount Jefferson, the victim of record January cold and wind.

That this sentinel of the North Country has succeeded this year
in taking the lives of a handful of new victims—the latest being 21-
year-old Cheryl Weingarten, a Tufts University student from Hew-
lett, New York—comes as no real surprise. Since October 19, 1849,
when 29-year-old Englishman Fred Strickland became the mountain's first victim after losing his way while descending the peak on
its western slopes, the mountain and the entire Presidential Range
have taken the lives of 114 people.

Some have been victims of hiking or skiing accidents. Others
have perished in train wrecks, airplane crashes, and carriage road
mishaps. All, of course, have contributed to the mountain's legacy
and mystique.

For more than a century, the mountain's reputation for torturous weather conditions and the toll the peak has taken on climbers have been well chronicled in print and been absorbed by millions of readers. The Rev. Thomas Starr King, in his classic 1859 book, *The White Hills: Their Legends, Landscape and Poetry*, wrote, "You know that suffering and death are giving Mount Washington a tragical celebrity." And in describing a summer hike to the mountain's summit, he added, "It was July in Gorham . . . and November at the apex."

Nineteenth-century writer Julius Ward, who authored in 1890, *The White Mountains: A Guide to Their Interpretation*, marveled at the wonders of climbing the mountain, saying, "The ascent is a hard and sharp climb, but the outlook upon the world, that enlarges with each step, is every moment more enrapturing."

He warned, though, "Ordinarily the ascent of a mountain gives pleasure, but Mount Washington is haughty in its mood and will encourage no familiarity. All the world may be at peace with the highest Powers, but not so the monarch of the hills. The clouds drop their fatness in rain or sleet at the slightest invitation, and the gentle susurrus of the valleys becomes on the mountain summit the trumpet blast that drives all the forces of the heavens before it. There are no adequate terms to describe a storm on Mount Washington. . . . Nothing but the mountain itself, weighted down with its millions of broken rocks, can survive the contest in which the strongest forces of Nature are engaged."

As the deaths and accidents have mounted over the years, much more, of course, has been written of the mountain's feistiness.

"A piece of recklessness on the part of a climber, an accident, and the remote chance of being overtaken by a storm are the causes of any peril which may be attached to the trip," observed Frederick Kilbourne in *Chronicles of the White Mountains*, published in 1916.

And in 1973, in his book *Ten Years on the Rock Pile*, weather observer Lee Vincent wrote, "In trying to convey the sense of what the mountain is all about, I hope to impress upon you all that it is not a peak to try and pit yourself against in order to have an ego trip."

Despite (and most likely because of) its notoriety, it is a certainty that Mount Washington will continue to draw thousands to its summit and subsidiary ridges.

Mike Pelchat, General Supervisor for the Northern Region state parks, which include Mount Washington State Park, noted earlier this week that a quarter million people a year visit the mountain's summit annually. Many reach the mountaintop by either the Auto Road or Cog Railway, while about 60,000 hike to the rocky summit.

Thousands of others pay visits to the mountain's lower flanks, perhaps to ice climb in the winter, or ski infamous Tuckerman Ravine in spring. Tuckerman's, which has claimed more than its share of victims over the years, in a single weekend day will draw as many as 3,600 skiers and spectators.

Appalachian Mountain Club spokesperson Rob Burbank adds that a quarter million people each year pass through the AMC's Pinkham Notch Visitor Center at the mountain's eastern base.

Dave Thurlow, a meteorologist for the nonprofit Mount Washington Observatory, said last week the fact that Mount Washington is the region's highest summit is surely the major reason why so many hikers make their way to the mountaintop summit each year. The mountain's unique summit community is also an attraction, said Thurlow.

Pelchat said the uniqueness of the Presidential Range's alpine zone is an added natural draw for hikers. That the mountain, like the entire White Mountain National Forest, is so close to the Eastern seaboard's huge population centers also makes it that much more accessible to literally millions of people; many of whom just aren't prepared for what the mountain has to offer.

Considering the large number of people who make their way by foot to the Rock Pile's top each year, Thurlow and others say Mount Washington isn't necessarily the fiend that everyone makes it out to be. "When you factor in how many people are killed or hurt every year, and compare that to the total number of visitors the mountain has, the ratio of deaths to hikers is pretty small," said Thurlow.

The majority of those who do run into trouble on the mountain are those trampers who are either inexperienced or are unfamiliar with the mountain's sometimes hostile environment.

"This mountain is unique in that its weather changes so dramatically in such a relatively short change in altitude," said Thurlow. Hikers working their way up the mountain below the treeline, he said, gain a false sense of security. When they finally do get above the treeline, and are greeted by fog, winds often in excess of 50 and 60 miles per hour, and anything else the mountain has to throw at them, they get into trouble.

"There are times when it's not safe to be on the mountain . . . and for those who do take on the mountain under those circumstances, that's when you're pushing the envelope," said Thurlow.

"You can be an extremely intelligent person, but in a mountain environment things are totally different," adds Pelchat, a veteran rescuer who has participated in more than his share of mountain dramatics.

The longtime Gorham resident said far too often hikers encountering trouble on Mount Washington don't know enough to retreat. "They seem to forget or don't understand that the higher up the mountain they go, the worse the conditions are going to be."

In summer especially, when the summit buildings are open to the traveling public, hikers are usually even more determined to make it to the top, even in deteriorating weather. "They figure once they reach the summit they'll be able to seek shelter. Unfortunately they aren't always able to make it that far," said Pelchat.

"There are times," adds AMC's Burbank, "when it makes sense to turn back. People have to come to grips with that."

Burbank said Monday that if anything good has come out of the recent spate of mountain accidents, it is the fact that the public is gaining through various media reports additional education on the potential perils of hiking Mount Washington and Presidential Range. "I think people are beginning to realize more and more that this isn't a mountain to trifle with," said Burbank. "Mount Washington can be a very safe place to be, if you approach things correctly. By the same token, as we have found out too many times already this year, it can be a deadly place to be as well."

The First Victim

It was the week after Columbus Day in 1849 when Englishman Frederick Strickland decided he just had to reach the summit of the greatest of the great White Hills.

As happens on occasion in the mountains of northern New England, and particularly along the mile-high Presidential Range, an early season snowfall had swept across the region, leaving a strong white reminder of what was to be in store for northern New Hampshire in the coming winter months. The snow, perhaps as deep as two or three feet in the higher elevations, loomed large as an obstacle to his planned climb.

Despite the urgings of innkeeper Thomas Crawford not to attempt the trek, Strickland insisted he could make it to Mount Washington's snow-covered summit, even if the horse he was to use for the first part of the ascent couldn't. So on the morning of October 19, Strickland, another Englishman, a guide, and several saddle horses began the long climb, setting out from Crawford's Notch House inn.

Slowly ploughing their way through the deepening snow, the group made it as far as Mount Pleasant (now known as Mount Eisenhower), where the snow was so deep the guide insisted he and his horses would go no further. Neither would the second Englishman.

Left to himself to complete the climb, Strickland proceeded slowly along the exposed southern Presidentials, and successfully reached Washington's cold, windswept summit, probably in early or midafternoon. On his way off the mountain, however, along the now abandoned Fabyan Path, he somehow lost his way in the deep snow, fell into a stream, discarded his frozen clothing, and stumbled a mile more. Two days later his badly bruised and lifeless body was found by searchers in the rocky bed of the Ammonoosuc River. Tragically, he had become notorious Mount Washington's first victim.

In the 145 years that have passed since that snowy October, many others have joined Strickland on Mount Washington's lengthy casualty list. According to the Appalachian Mountain Club, one of several keepers of the death list, 114 people have lost their lives on Mount Washington and the Presidential Range; most on Washington's various slopes.

While Strickland's death was the first such reported tragedy on the mountain, his passing has never received the notoriety of the mountain's second victim, 23-year-old Lizzie Bourne; the Kennebunkport, Maine woman whose life was taken away September 13, 1855 after she was overcome by cold and exhaustion just a few hundred feet from the safety of the summit's mid-19th century mountaintop buildings.

Bourne's death, which at the time received much newspaper play throughout New England, has been immortalized over the years by the placement of a monument at the spot where she died.

The mountain's early victims also include Ewald Weiss, 24, of Berlin, Germany, who on August 24, 1890 left the Summit House for a hike to Mount Adams, the 5,774-foot peak of the northern Presidentials, and second highest mountain in all of New England.

Whether Weiss ever made it to Adams was never determined as once he left Washington's summit he was never seen again.

The same fate was apparently met by surveyor John M. Keenan, 18, of Charlestown, Massachusetts. On September 18, 1912, he too wandered off Washington's rocky cone. And like Weiss, no one saw him again.

The greatest mass casualty incident on Mount Washington occurred on September 17, 1967, when a Cog Railway train derailed and crashed, killing eight passengers and injuring more than 70 others. Thirty-eight years earlier, a Boston photographer covering the final mountain run of the Cog's renovated old engine, Peppersass, died when the train engine careened out of control while descending the railway line.

The mountain's lower reaches have also proven to be unforgiving as no less than four persons have died in drowning accidents. Glen House proprietor J. M. Thompson was the first drowning victim on October 4, 1869 as he was swept away by the rising waters of the flooded Peabody River.

In 1927 a woodsman lost his life in swollen Jefferson Brook as he was checking his trap lines.

Eerie Evidence

It is a strange coincidence that several of the mountain's life-snatching incidents have been so similar. The May 1 death of Weingarten, the 21-year-old Tufts University student, is eerie evidence of that.

Rescue officials say Weingarten was headed down off the mountain, after successfully summiting the peak, when she slipped and fell on the hard-packed slopes just above the lip of Tuckerman Ravine. Unable to arrest her fall, Weingarten slid into the 60-foot deep crevasse—created annually by a running, year-round brook—and landed on a rock, breaking her neck on impact.

On May 1, 1949, exactly 45 years earlier, Dr. Paul Schiller of Orange Park, Florida—a psychologist doing work for Harvard University—was skiing near the top of Tuckerman's headwall when he apparently slipped, fell and slid 50 feet into a crevasse. The crevasse was the same one Weingarten fell into two weeks ago, and according to Pelchat, a veteran of many rescue operations on the Presidential Range, the rock the Tufts University student struck was the same that killed Schiller. For many years, in fact, the rock has been known as Schiller Rock.

In May of 1972, a 21-year-old Yale University student, Christopher Coyne of New Haven, Connecticut, was attempting to descend on snowshoes via the Tuckerman headwall when he apparently took a spill, lost control, slid down the icy slopes and fell 40 feet into the base of a waterfall. If you hadn't guessed by now, it was in the same spot where Schiller and Weingarten had fallen. It took six days for searchers to discover Coyne's body, and an heroic effort by a band of rescuers to retrieve his body from its wet, rocky and hidden resting place.

Tuckerman Ravine, of course, has climbed many other lives over the years; some of them skiers, who unsuccessfully took on the ravine's famous headwall, and others like Philip Longnecker, 25, of Toledo, Ohio and Jacques Parysko, 23, of Cambridge, Massachusetts, who froze to death on a winter camping trip in late January 1954.

Next to Tuckerman's, Huntington Ravine, a mecca for rock and ice climbers, is the mountain's second deadliest area. Its first victim was a 19-year-old Cambridge, Massachusetts man who was killed by a falling stone on September 18, 1931.

In late January of 1969, Huntington Ravine took three lives in one fell swoop. Scot Stevens, 19, of Cucamonga, California, Robert Ellenberg, 19, of New York City, and Charles Yoder, 24, of Hartford, Wisconsin were ice climbing together in the ravine when authorities believe they fell, roped together, some 1,200 feet to their deaths.

This year already, Mount Washington and the Presidential Range have claimed four more lives, including those of two men who froze to death at the top of Huntington Ravine. Considering that the number of deaths over the last several decades has averaged somewhere around one and a half a year, 1994 has produced more than its share of tragedies in its first five months. As Pelchat said last week, "We're tired of hauling (dead) bodies off the mountain."

It would be foolish, of course, to believe that since the mountain has taken more than its share of lives this year, it will now let down its defenses for a few months and let all those who proceed over its slopes, do so safely.

Mount Washington's track record is such that no one should ever take this rock pile for granted. Anyone who does is assuredly a candidate to be victim No. 115.

A Winter Weekend
Atop the Rock Pile

January 8 and 15, 1997

Stepping outside the main entrance to the Sherman Adams Summit Building atop Mount Washington, I gingerly made my way across the slushy ice and snow that covered the 6,288-foot peak.

By Mount Washington's standards, it was downright balmy on the summit, with the temperature a mild 32 degrees. A few miles below the mountain, at its eastern base in Pinkham Notch, the thermometer showed a reading of 31 degrees.

Overnight, as a warm front moved across New England, temperatures actually rose on the mountaintop, and with the rise came thick clouds, tropical storm force winds, and sheets of rain.

Dressed up in every bit of foul weather gear I possessed, I (along with several other intrepid summit visitors) cautiously proceeded forward in the rain, wind and fog, ever mindful of the icy mess under foot. With visibility reduced to less than 100 feet in the soup-like fog, and winds gusting to as high as 74 miles an hour, none of us dared venture too far from the main summit building for fear we'd never find it again.

Our mission for the moment was to attempt to get photographs of the inhospitable mountaintop. Instead, most of our cameras remained secure within the relative safety of our pile jackets and Gore-Tex rain gear. It was no day for pictures atop Mount Washington.

Ten minutes after venturing out into the exposed, wild elements of the mountain, our entire group—now sopping wet from the wind-driven rain—was back inside the chilled, unheated main floor of the summit building. As we unbuckled our crampons and doffed

A winter tramper reaches the upper end of the Tuckerman Ravine Trail near the summit of Mount Washington.

our soaked apparel, we didn't need to be reminded that we were atop the home of the "World's Worst Weather."

My recent visit to the summit was courtesy of the Mount Washington Observatory, which for more than 60 years has operated the summit weather station now housed in the Sherman Adams Building. I was amongst a group of eight people taking part in a weekend Alpine Photography workshop offered by the Observatory.

Like all of the Observatory's winter EduTrip workshops, the program included a night's stay atop the mountain in the cozy headquarters of the weather observers. Transportation to and from the summit was provided by the Observatory's Sno-Cat, which on Saturday had delivered us to the summit from Pinkham Notch in about 90 minutes driving time up the famed Mount Washington Auto Road.

Scheduling and planning a winter trip to the summit is hardly a sure thing in midwinter, as any winter tramper can attest. In the case of the EduTrips, prevailing weather conditions dictate whether or not the Sno-Cat can make it up the Auto Road and deliver participants to the top of the Rock Pile, as Mount Washington is sometimes called. As the folks who run the Observatory well know, a successful ascent one day brings no guarantee that a safe trip down will be in the offing the next day, or really anytime soon.

The weekend focus for our group was on photography, and specifically alpine photography for the hiker and mountaineer. Our instructor was none other than Ned Therrien, the retired U.S. Forest Service ranger from Gilford who now works as a professional photographer, taking pictures for magazines, books, and numerous corporate clients. Co-leading the trip was one of the Observatory's staff photographers.

With cloudy conditions and wet weather forecast for both Saturday and Sunday, conditions certainly weren't optimal for the two-day workshop, at least not if we planned on honing our photo skills in the usually spectacular winter environs of the Presidential Range. Knowing quite well Mount Washington's reputation for dastardly winter weather, I certainly figured the odds were against us getting decent photo weather. Facts are facts, and this is a peak that on average is covered in clouds and fog (from sunrise to sunset) 21 out of 31 days each January.

As we began our trek up the Auto Road at 9 a.m. Saturday, the encouraging word from weather observers on the summit was that the mountaintop was clear of fog and clouds, and that a brilliant undercast (where the cloud cover lay well below the elevation of the summit) prevailed. These conditions would likely hold for the morning and into the afternoon. By night, though, clouds and rain were expected to move into the region.

For the first half of the eight-mile trek up the snow-covered Auto Road, there was no indication that we'd ever break out of the clouds and fog. But shortly after passing the halfway point, glimpses of the Northern Peaks of the Presidential Range were offered through slight breaks in the cloud cover. And by the time we'd covered five miles of the road, we too were above the clouds, staring wondrously up at snowclad Mounts Jefferson, Adams and Madison to the north.

The further up the Auto Road we went, the greater the spectacle. Rime ice and frost feathers coated every rock and tree in sight. Above the heavy bank of clouds were also seen the very tops of some of the White Mountains' highest peaks. To the east, directly across Pinkham Notch, was impressive Carter Dome. Well to the west could be seen the alpine summits of Franconia Ridge. Barely recognizable, though, were the tracks of the Cog Railway, cloaked in a foot or more of rime ice, while the clouds well below us prevented any glimpses of the towns and villages so often shadowed by this behemoth of a mountain.

With temperatures in the mid-20s and winds practically nonexistent at the summit—a true rarity at this or any other time of the year—the setting proved ideal for a hands-on photo workshop, and for some three hours we wandered around and near the summit, aiming our cameras on hikers climbing the mountain by trail, on an off-duty Observatory crew member whisking his way down the Auto Road on a plastic sled, and on the dramatic landscape of the Presidential Range peaks and others beyond.

I'd be hard pressed to recall a summit visit I've experienced that was more exhilarating, more intoxicating than that of Saturday. It was the type of day you didn't want to see end, even though you knew the sunset that we'd soon be witnessing would be something else to behold.

On my one other winter visit to the top of Mount Washington—on a cold and clear day in March 1988—I was too weary from the long hike up the mountain, and too chilled by the wind, to really

Distant peaks and ridgelines poke through the undercast to provide a dramatic panorama from the top of Mount Washington.

soak in the beauty of this peak in its midwinter glory. But this time around things were different

Instead of fumbling around in the numbing cold for that extra layer of clothing, on this visit I got to see the mountain for what it can occasionally be—a winter treat with a humane heart.

Forget for a moment the tragedies that too often are associated with this mountain. Forget too that a quarter million people a year visit the summit—mostly by train or automobile. And forget about the mountain's ferocious weather. When conditions are right, as they were on this day, Mount Washington can be as lovely and intriguing as any peak in New England. Minus the chaotic summit scenes of summer and fall, this mountain is really special. Unfortunately that's a sentiment that has too often escaped me in the past

The much anticipated sunset capped off our outdoor ventures for the day, and what a sunset it was! Through the sea of clouds still cloaking the landscape to the west, distant peaks resembled islands. And all around these island peaks, the sea of clouds glowed orange as the setting sun reflected its dying light off their tops.

Before retiring into the bowels of the Sherman Adams building for an evening of conversation, more photo talk, and a family-style dinner with 16 other mountain souls, I joined Observatory education program coordinator Peter Crane for a quick visit to the round observation tower at the northwest corner of the concrete summit structure. As day faded into night, and the clouds began to break up in the valleys, the lights of Bretton Woods Ski Area and nearby Twin Mountain village twinkled in the distance. Later we'd spot lights from what seemed to be a thousand little towns and cities, including Portland, Maine, 65 miles or so to the east.

And as I looked out the window from the weather observers' offices upstairs in the summit building, I waved quietly in the direction of my hometown, Littleton, where my wife, I suspected, was probably wondering how her husband was faring at the home of the "World's Worst Weather."

At that moment, I was fine. After a day like we'd had atop Mount Washington, there was no other way to be.

Life Atop Mount Washington

On a normal winter day atop Mount Washington, a half dozen people—and sometimes more—call the mountain their home.

Staff members and interns of the nonprofit Mount Washington Observatory have been staffing the summit weather observatory for some 65 years. They live and work on the mountain 24 hours a day, seven days a week. Through rain, snow, fog and winds often in excess of 100 miles per hour, these people monitor the mountain's infamous weather extremes, and work on various other scientific projects, many of them related to the cold.

As I found out on my recent weekend venture to the summit, everyday life is far from normal on top of a mountain which this time of year can rightfully claim to be home to the "World's Worst Weather." Obviously prevailing weather conditions account mainly for the unusual lifestyle endured by Observatory crew members and summit visitors like myself.

As workshop participants are reminded when signing up for one of the Observatory's popular winter EduTrip workshops, an average midwinter day on Mount Washington finds the summit encrusted in rime-ice producing fog, with visibility limited to 100 feet or less. The average temperature is only four degrees Fahrenheit, while winds are generally 50 miles an hour (with gusts of 70 mph or more likely most every day). The low temperatures and cold winter winds produce a daily wind chill approaching minus-50 degrees.

As for snowfall, well the records speak for themselves. The summit receives an average of 40 inches or more a month from December through March. In a year, the mountain will see a little more than 250 inches, with December and March typically the snowiest months (averaging 42.6 and 42.5 inches respectively).

In an environment such as this, summit residents spend most of their time hunkered down in the Observatory's headquarters in the Sherman Adams Summit Building, built by the state and opened for occupation in 1980. The modern, concrete structure—-the Observatory's sixth mountaintop home—-with its trademark weather observer's tower on its west end, is eerily cold and quiet in winter and is bereft of the thousands of tourists and hikers who flock to the northeast's highest mountain during the busy summer and fall months.

On a mountaintop that can be as cold and inhospitable as any place on earth, heat is a precious commodity, and only where it is necessary will you find it. The bulk of the summit structure is minimally heated in winter, with the temperature either a few degrees below or barely above freezing for the most part. Where the observers work, eat and sleep is kept at a comfortably warm 69 degrees (or at least it was on my visit).

The Observatory occupies just a small portion of the building, that being the two floors nearest to the tower. The observers' working quarters are situated on the main floor of the Sherman Adams Building, past the post office and snack bar areas frequented by warm weather summit visitors. Downstairs are the living quarters for the Observatory's crew members.

Weather, naturally, predominates everywhere in the Observatory. Upstairs, in the work area, where banks of computers and other monitoring devices line both walls of a long, narrow room, observers watch the weather both through the instrumentation readings and by peering out several small windows. Downstairs, in the living quarters, computer monitors detail the current wind and temperature conditions every minute, showing readings both for the summit and the valley far below in Pinkham Notch.

Crew members, both those on and off duty, stay atop the summit for a week at a time, splitting their hours between work, rest, and minimal play (at least in winter). The regular Observatory crew members are assisted by several interns (usually college students), making for a total of five or six workers on the mountain at once.

The Observatory crew generally doesn't worry about cooking meals, since those duties are usually performed by volunteers who also come to the summit for a week at a time to do their part for the organization. According to longtime Observatory staffer Ken Rancourt, "the volunteers are expected to make our meals, but those of us on the summit are expected to help in the cleanup."

With the advent of the winter EduTrip program several winters ago, the mountain observatory isn't as quiet as it once was. Between staff members, interns, volunteers, workshop participants, and others, it's not unusual to find 15 to 20 people on the mountain at one time. Rancourt said there's bunk space for as many as 24 in the building, but a good number of those available bunks are in the unheated portion of the summit building, where the weekend I was on the mountain the temperature in the bunk area was a refreshing 36 degrees. The people who bunk out in this area are rooming with much of the Observatory's perishable food items, which are kept on a large counter and table, just as if they were inside a walk-in refrigerator.

It's one thing to be atop Mount Washington in the summer, when trains and motor vehicles can make it to the summit on most any day. It's quite another to be here in winter, when the only mechanized transportation to and from the valley is the Observatory's Sno-Cat, which typically makes the climb two or three times a week. You never know from one day to the next whether your ride will be able to reach the summit from Pinkham. Overnight EduTrippers aren't guaranteed a ride down the mountain either; that's why no one is taken to the summit this time of year without being fully equipped for extensive above treeline winter travel. When really bad weather strikes, observers (and others) stay the course, whether their seven-day tour of duty is up or the weekend workshop has concluded. They get down off the mountain when they can, and are almost always at nature's whims.

The isolation of the summit, and its harsh environment, presents challenges to all who live, work or visit the summit Observatory in winter. For instance, there are no power lines or water lines to the mountaintop. Instead, generators owned by Channel 8 television—which has its transmitter on the summit, along with a year-round manned facility—provide expensive (28 cents a kilowatt hour) electricity to the Summit Building. Water, meanwhile, is drawn from a well 800 feet deep, well below the line of permafrost found at this elevation.

The economics of keeping the Observatory running demand that power be used sparingly. Visitors are reminded constantly to use lights and other electric-powered devices only when necessary. Water, though maybe not in short supply, is always a concern too. If the well and/or its pump fails, it's not like you can call a repairmen to the summit to fix things; not when its 10 below zero and winds are blasting away at the Rock Pile with hurricane force. Fresh water is also transported to the summit to supplement the well water. Toilets are flushed infrequently, to both save on water and save capacity in the summit building's septic system, which can't be emptied until spring.

Did I mention also that there's only one working toilet in the place? You find out quickly that the bathroom is about the busiest place on the summit when there's a crowd of 17 people in the building with you.

Unless the weather is optimum, and outdoor travel is safe, summit residents and visitors tend to stick close to home on their infrequent excursions outside the building. Until you've been outdoors on this mountaintop, on a cold, windy, foggy and snowy (or rainy) day in winter, you can't possibly imagine how easy it is to lose one's sense of place even on a peak that is crowded with a half dozen buildings and a slew of communication towers. The mountaintop takes on a ghostlike appearance with its many buildings cloaked in rime ice and the fog and snow blurring one's perspective. The building can be there in front of you one moment, and gone the next. Getting lost—quickly—is a very real possibility.

It's a different story, of course, on days when the mountain is more hospitable to above treeline travel. The weather observers enjoy the mountain as much as anyone. I got to see one observer begin a six-mile descent on the Auto Road on a red plastic sled. He covered that distance in a mere 15 minutes, then hiked his way back to the summit to tell of his sledding feat. Peter Crane boasts that an Observatory staffer is also credited with being the first person to snowboard his way off the summit several seasons ago.

Certainly there is nothing normal about life on Mount Washington. Not in summer, and definitely not in winter. Yet it's a strange but wonderful place to call home, even if it's only for a night.

Jeremy Haas Recounts Mountain Tragedy

November 30, 1994

Under ordinary circumstances, Jeremy Haas' winter mountaineering experiences of nearly a year ago would have awed most people.

Battling winds of 70–80 miles an hour and temperatures 30 to 40 degrees below zero, the 20-year-old Haas miraculously stumbled and crawled his way safely through the snow and up and over the rocky landscape of the Presidential Range to the top Mount Washington, the region's highest and most famous summit.

By the time he reached Washington's summit, his exposed hands were frozen into a tight ball, relegating them virtually useless, and he was showing signs of hypothermia. For 30 minutes he rapped loudly on a door to one of the summit buildings, hoping to gain the attention of Mount Washington Observatory crew members inside. For the longest time, no one answered his knocks.

Finally, an observer inside realized that the rapping sounds he and others had heard weren't weather-related noises, but man-made. In the darkness of a midwinter night atop the mountain known worldwide for its fierce weather, the observer spotted Haas and shortly thereafter he was safely inside the observatory.

No one will ever question the stamina, fortitude and toughness of Haas, now a 21-year-old senior at the University of New Hampshire, for few have ever survived a mountain ordeal like this. Mere mortals have passed on under far better weather conditions. His climb was truly remarkable and memorable.

What Haas will forever be known for, however, is not his valiant January 1994 winter ascent of Mount Washington, as incredible as it may seem. Instead, Haas will go down in White Mountains hiking annals as the college kid who didn't know when to stop. He was the man, people will recall, who let his hiking companion, 21-year-old Derek Tinkham, freeze to death on the exposed ridgeline between Mount Washington and neighboring Mount Jefferson.

In the days after the highly publicized mid-January tragedy on the Presidential Range, Jeremy Haas' own words to the media embittered the northern New England mountain climbing world. Haas spoke of the challenge and excitement of tackling the mountains in extreme weather conditions. He talked of winter mountaineering as being essentially a solo effort, not a team effort. And he talked about getting "near the edge of life and death." But there were few, if any, words of sorrow or remorse.

The public, including many in the climbing world, decried Haas as being an overzealous, headstrong individual whose unwarranted risks not only cost one young winter hiker his life, but also placed in extreme peril the lives of a dozen or more volunteer rescuers, who were called upon to take to the slopes of Mount Jefferson to retrieve Tinkham's frozen, body.

In the months since January's much publicized mountain incident, Haas, now just a few short months from getting his degree from UNH, has recovered physically from the ordeal, which left him with severely frostbitten hands. In fact, he heads to the mountains practically every free weekend, either to take on a White Mountains peak by trail, or to rock climb his way up a crag or cliff face.

The physical part of the recovery, in many ways, however, has been much easier than the mental part. For leaving a friend to die on a mountain is not something that is easily forgotten; not by one's self, nor by those who have read and heard about the mountain tragedy.

"It's a complex situation . . . I'm still trying to figure it all out myself," said Haas last week during a visit to a social studies class at Profile Junior High in Bethlehem. "I expect some criticism . . . and much of it is deserved. We made some mistakes."

Haas was invited to speak to the Profile students by junior high student Robert Parish of Franconia, who for a class assignment recently read the book *Second Ascent*, the biography of climber Hugh Herr, who in January 1982 lost his way while attempting a climb to Mount Washington's summit. Herr and his climbing partner, Jeff Batzer, both survived a three-day ordeal in the wintry woods just north of the mountain, but a member of the North Conway-based Mountain Rescue Service, 28-year-old Albert Dow of Tuftonboro, lost his life when he was swept several hundred feet down the mountain by an avalanche and smashed against a tree, instantly dying in the impact.

Haas, who attends school at UNH with Parish's older sister, said his mountain ordeal last winter was similar in ways to Herr's, though surely not exactly alike. Both encountered bad winter weather, of course, and both incidents resulted in unfortunate deaths. But Herr, said Haas, probably endured as much, if not more criticism from the public, since his mountain odyssey resulted in the death of one of the North Country's very own—a volunteer rescuer who gave his life to save the life of two climbers who made careless mistakes on a mountain that is rarely forgiving in midwinter.

"Hugh Herr's accident touched the locals because it involved one of their own, not just some climber up from the flatlands," said Haas. The criticisms he has endured over 10 months time would have been even greater, he speculated, if similar circumstances had arisen last winter.

A Tragic Decision

Most veteran winter climbers will agree that Haas, from Ithaca, New York, and Tinkham, a Rhode Islander, had no business being on the Presidential Range last January, not with record cold temperatures and high winds in the forecast. To undertake a traverse of the Presidential Range under those conditions is foolhardy and practically suicidal.

On the first day of their trek, Haas recalled that he and Tinkham hiked up Mount Madison and successfully bedded down for the night in bivouac bags. The next day they planned to continue south along the ridge, over Mounts Adams and Jefferson, then set up camp in Sphinx Col—the low spot between Jefferson and Washington.

Despite frigid temperatures and harsh, biting winds, the pair made it up to Mount Adams' summit, then headed further along the Gulfside Trail towards Jefferson. Along the way they passed by several connecting trails leading down to lean-tos and cabins below treeline and sheltered from the elements.

The critical decision that ultimately led to Tinkham's death was made at Edmands Col, the low point between Adams and Madison.

At that point, Haas and Tinkham could have retreated off the ridge-line and sought shelter at one of several nearby Randolph Mountain Club shelters. Instead, they decided to forge onward to Mount Jefferson and Sphinx Col.

Looking back now at that fateful moment, Haas said he failed to recognize then that his climbing partner was beginning to be overcome by hypothermia, and thus was not able to make rational decisions. By the time he sensed Derek was in trouble, it was too late to do anything about it.

"Derek was unable to make the proper decision for himself at that point. The decision I made to continue on was the wrong one," admitted Haas.

As the two began the arduous ascent of Mount Jefferson, Tinkham became noticeably weaker. Soon the two reached the point of no return.

"On the climb up (to Jefferson), we had the wind at our backs. I thought of retracing our steps back to (Edmands Col), but that would have put us going straight into the wind. I'm not sure either of us could have done that, plus we were only a half hour away from our camp site."

Haas said Tinkham focused whatever energy he had left on reaching Jefferson's summit. From there, it would be a 15-minute walk to Sphinx Col, where the two planned to bivouac for the night. But the climb up Mount Jefferson apparently sapped Tinkham of all his reserves, and by the time the two had reached the col, Tinkham's physical condition had deteriorated to the point where Haas suspected his friend would not survive the night.

"In this type of expedition, you need to have some reserve energy stored up inside you . . . to deal with the unexpected. Derek used his up getting to Jefferson's summit. He had nothing left after that."

Fearful for his own life now, Haas said he then had to confront his partner with the seriousness of the situation. "I gave him the choice to either make one attempt to get down below treeline, or to stay in the col for the night. I told him I didn't think I could take care of both him and myself. He chose to stay where he was, and I chose to head to the summit of Mount Washington. Under the circumstances, that was probably the best thing to do. If I'd stayed, there probably would have been two dead people up there."

Haas said he did his best to bundle Tinkham up for the night, but in reality, he knew Derek's chances of survival were slim. Haas said he takes some solace in knowing that physicians, who asked him about Tinkham's condition later, concurred that Derek's condition "was probably irreversible" when he left him.

Haas described his three-mile walk to Mount Washington's as "the longest four hours of his life." He expected the trek would take an hour, maybe two, but he was forced to crawl on his hands and knees at times to avoid the ferocious summit winds.

To make matters worse, Haas said his hands were frozen into a fist and had been that way since he left Tinkham and Sphinx Col. He had taken his gloves off while readying Tinkham for his night on the mountain. His hands froze nearly instantly in the bitter cold conditions, and he was unable to place them back into his gloves.

Atop Washington's summit he was assisted by Observatory workers and a doctor and nurse, who just happened to be on the mountain for the weekend. Continued cold and windy weather squelched any immediate plans to have Haas taken off the mountain for much needed medical treatment. Instead he would remain at the Observatory for several extra days, until conditions improved enough that the Observatory's Thiokol snow machine could safely descend the mountain to Pinkham Notch.

Risky Rescue Mission

The day following his ascent of Washington, rescuers made a bold and daring climb up Jefferson to find Tinkham. Although his chances for survival were slim, rescuers held out hope that perhaps by some miracle he was still alive.

Haas said last week the decision to send search teams onto the Range was risky, and perhaps unwarranted under the conditions. "It was a difficult, largely unnecessary rescue," said Haas. That's not to say he doesn't appreciate what the rescuers went through—especially under the prevailing weather conditions—but was it worth it, he asked, to imperil other people's lives in a situation that he viewed as hopeless?

Much of the criticism flung at him since last winter is justifiable, admits Haas. He said he wishes now he could take back some of the things he said to the media in the days after the accident. "I brought on a lot by myself," he said, by first saying the wrong things, and then shutting out the media entirely.

Haas said he was hurt by some of the inaccurate stories that surfaced about previous winter hikes he had taken. Particularly bothersome was the story that on a previous Presidential Range hike, a companion of his lost all 10 of his toes to frostbite. "That is totally false. The guy didn't lose any toes, and he still hikes in the mountains."

The allure of hiking the mountains in less than ideal conditions remains with Haas, despite last winter's incident. "I like the nasty weather. It's fun being out in it, because it's not something a lot of people get to see or experience."

He debunks the notion that he and his climbing partner were out of their league in tackling the Presidential Range last winter. He said Tinkham was a good, strong hiker, and also a "smart guy, an EMT."

"Where I went wrong," said Haas, "was in believing that my winter hiking and camping experience would make up for Derek's inexperience."

Although there is an unwritten code in the mountain climbing community that when a climber gets in trouble, there will be people out there available to come to his or her aid, Haas knows he pushed everyone to the limit last winter.

He has read all the negative comments in the newspapers, and been told in writing that "the wrong person" died on the mountain in January. "I know I need to pay back some debts to the mountaineering community . . . I need to make a contribution in some way."

Talking about last year's tragic events to a group of Profile Junior High students was a start in that direction, but it will be a long time before all the debts are paid.

In the meantime, no one will forget what happened to Hass last January on Mount Washington, nor will they soon forgive him. That's one price Jeremy Haas will be paying for a long time to come.

Tuckerman Ravine:
A Spring Phenomenon

April 9, 1997

Like nowhere else in the East, Tuckerman Ravine has a reputation that most definitely precedes itself.

Whether you're a hiker, a skier, or a home body whose idea of outdoor exercise is strolling from the front porch to the front seat of the car, everyone knows about Tuckerman Ravine and its legendary status as king of the backcountry ski scene.

The bowl-shaped glacial cirque on the southeast shoulder of Mount Washington is the mecca of the Northeast when it comes to spring skiing. For decades, skiers have trekked several thousand feet up to its lofty heights and dared to challenge its steep headwall and lip, with grades as high as 55 degrees.

The spring scene at Tuckerman Ravine is nothing short of a phenomenon. On a warm weekend day in late April or early May, when the changing of the seasons has turned decidedly in spring's favor, thousands of people will hike three miles or more for one last taste of winter.

Many will be seen lugging their downhill skis and ski boots up the wide Tuckerman Ravine hiking trail in preparation for their schuss of Left Gully, The Lip, or the snow-covered headwall. Others will be seen with snowboards, sleds, or their telemark skis. Still others will be carrying nothing but their hiking packs. They have come to the ravine simply to soak in the radiant sunshine and bask in the spectacle that is spring skiing at Tuck's.

Probably no one knows the Ravine like Brad Ray, the U.S. Forest Service worker who has patrolled this area of Mount Washington since 1959. As lead snow ranger on the White Mountain National Forest, Ray has seen it all, done it all, and heard it all.

"You're never perfectly safe in Tuckerman Ravine," said Ray last weekend as he stood at the base of Tuckerman's bowl, watching the season's first major onslaught of spring skiers. "We have falling rocks, falling ice, falling snow, and falling people. There's an awful lot of falling that goes on around here. That's one reason why this place can be so dangerous."

Tuckerman Ravine and Mount Washington are no stranger to danger and tragedy, that's for sure. While the winter of 1996–97 has been relatively quiet, at least in terms of major skiing or hiking accidents on the mountain, Ray remembers all too well last winter, when the mountain known worldwide for its hazards claimed the lives of five people. Deaths in Tuckerman Ravine or in several of the mountain's other glacially-carved ravines have claimed a large percentage of the 120-some odd lives that have been lost on the Presidential Range in the last 150 years.

Ray, one of four snow rangers presently working on the White Mountain National Forest, said his primary job, and the job of the other rangers, is to assess snow conditions in the ravines and to make a determination whether or not severe avalanche danger exists. Following several avalanche-related deaths a year ago on the mountain, Ray and the Forest Service go to great lengths to keep hikers and skiers informed of prevailing snow conditions in all of the mountain's avalanche prone areas. Of course they can't stop anyone from proceeding into areas where the avalanche risk is high, but they can strongly advise these same people what they should and should not be attempting.

The snow rangers are generally the first humans to visit Tuckerman or nearby Huntington Ravine each morning, almost always well before the first hiker or skier has made his or her way up into the ravines from AMC's Pinkham Notch Visitor Center. "We get into the ravines as early as possible to check on the snow conditions. We need to be accurate, though, so sometimes it may take us longer than usual. Once we've made our determination, the information is sent down the mountain and it is provided to 20 different outlets across the region," explained Ray. Naturally one of those outlets is AMC's base facility in Pinkham Notch, where from mid-March to mid-May each year, every person headed into the Ravine is legally obligated to begin their trek.

Several years back, recalled Ray, the Forest Service fought off efforts to make the Ravine more accessible to skiers by banning helicopter and train excursions to the summit. "It was our opinion, and the opinion of many people that we talked to, that we should preserve tradition and only allow access to the Ravine by way of the hiking trail," said Ray. "We think it's important that skiers walk up what they're going to be skiing down."

According to Marianne Bradley, the first and only female snow ranger to work in the Ravine, the threat from avalanches is very real on the Presidential Range and Mount Washington. In 1996, three hikers on the mountain were buried alive by avalanches—one on the Lion Head hiking trail and two in the Gulf of Slides. Bradley said a person buried by an avalanche has just a 50 percent chance of survival if they haven't been found within 30 minutes. The survival rate continues to decrease the longer one is under the snow.

During the spring ski season at Tuckerman's—a season that generally runs from the beginning of April through the end of May—the snow rangers are joined in the Ravine by staff members of the Appalachian Mountain Club and also members of the Mount Washington Volunteer Ski Patrol. Together, these three factions work hand in hand in greeting skiers, hikers and other visitors to the Ravine, answering questions, observing what's going on in the vicinity, and offering first aid to accident victims.

Bradley, her fellow snow rangers, and others who work in the Ravine, are all trained in avalanche rescue work and many are skilled in alpine mountaineering. When the rangers head into Tuckerman or Huntington Ravine to check on snow conditions, they do so armed with gear and equipment that would be useful in the event of an avalanche. Items like shovels and radio transceivers are a part of their arsenal.

Avalanches occur on steep slopes covered with unstable snow. They usually take place during or right after a snowstorm, but depending on weather conditions, the risk of avalanches may persist for several days

Unlike some adventurous mountain visitors, who sometimes fail to heed warnings of high avalanche danger, Bradley said that's

Skiers head into snow-covered Tuckerman Ravine as the 1997 spring ski season gets under way in the famous glacial cirque on the southeast slopes of Mount Washington.

something you won't catch her doing. "If there's a high risk of avalanche, I won't go into the Ravine," she said.

Of course avalanches aren't the only threat to human visitors to Tuckerman Ravine. Falling ice is also a threat to skiers, hikers and casual visitors. Ice blocks as big as cars and weighing as much as five tons have been known to break off the craggy cliffs hanging over and around the bowl. "I've seen these blocks of ice come sliding down, hit a boulder in the ravine and splinter like shrapnel," said Ray. "Falling ice is a very real threat, especially as the spring ski season goes on and the ice begins to melt. About all you can do is seek cover behind the largest rock you can find and hope for the best."

On a typical spring weekend when weather conditions are good, upwards of 3,000 people will trek into Tuckerman's to ski, hike, or just be there. One of them is Sheila Curtis of Woodstock, Maine, a member of the volunteer ski patrol at Tuckerman's for the last eight years. Like many of the recreational skiers who visit the Ravine annually, she's lured to the mountain by the challenge. "I'm a hard core skier. It's the attitude of this place that attracts me and a lot of other people like me."

For the most part, said Curtis, skiers play it safe in the Ravine, "But sometimes they do get out of control . . . they don't use prudence. I've seen a lot of craziness up here, like the time these six Ivy League students decided to come over Center Headwall on an inner tube. But I've seen a lot of skilled skiers here too. This place draws them all."

It was just over two years ago that Curtis lived perhaps the worst nightmare imaginable for a Tuckerman ski patroller. On a late March afternoon she watched longtime friend Chris Schneider, 32, of Pittsfield, Vermont fall at the top of a run down Hillman's Highway, slide head first into some rocks, and die on the spot. A day after the tragic ski run, she forced herself back up to Tuckerman Ravine and hiked to the top of Hillman's. "It was a way for me to deal with what happened. It was my way of coping with the loss of someone I really cared a lot about."

With the Forest Service facing major budget cuts the next few years, there's a strong possibility that the snow ranger force working on Mount Washington will be cut in half by the year 2000, said Ray. Should that happen, there's a concern that ongoing educational efforts will have to be curtailed and visitors to the mountain's ravines would be at greater risk.

A new organization, "Friends of Tuckerman," is being formed to help take up some of the expected slack, said Ray. The group will do some fund-raising and conduct mountain safety workshops, he said. "Getting this group up and running is one way for us to maintain what we have in terms of getting [the safety] message out. It's something that has to be done based on what we see happening down the road in a few years."

As for this year, it looks as though the Tuckerman ski season will be a lengthy one as parts of the Ravine's bowl remain buried under nearly 60 feet of snow. "The season is really just starting. April 1 is kind of the unofficial start," said snow ranger Chris Joosen. "The fun is just beginning."

Taking Issue

Preserving Our
Cultural Heritage

July 27, 1994

When we think of the U.S. Forest Service and its role in managing our cherished White Mountain National Forest, timber sales, hiking trails and ski area expansions are more likely to come to mind than archaeological digs or the preservation of cultural resources.

While controversies over clearcutting sections of the forest, or allowing ski areas like Loon Mountain to expand, garner the big headlines in daily and weekly newspapers across the state, the role the Forest Service plays in seeing that our cultural heritage is preserved is a low-key, unsensational task.

In recent years, though, the Forest Service has stepped up its efforts to identify and preserve for future generations the rich cultural heritage that this region possesses. Routinely, Forest Service personnel tramp through the pathless woods in search of artifacts or evidence that might provide a clue to a specific locale's past. That might mean searching for abandoned logging camps, following long idle logging railroad beds, seeking 16th- or 17th-century Native American settlements, or identifying closed or abandoned hiking trails.

It is important, says Jefferson forester Dave Govatski, that users of the National Forest work with the Forest Service to maintain and preserve the cultural heritage of the White Mountains. Persons who remove from the forest artifacts such as rusting saw blades or century-old railroad spikes are referred to as "time bandits" by forest personnel. "By removing items like these from the forest, they are depriving future generations of viewing these same things," says Govatski.

A few weeks back, Govatski, WMNF archaeologist Karl Roenke,

and cultural resource paraprofessional Jim Hill hosted a workshop
which brought more than a dozen participants to the historic Zealand Village area of Carroll. The workshop, cosponsored by the Appalachian Mountain Club, included an archaeological tour of the
Zealand area, with ventures to old building sites and along the aging
grade of the former Zealand Valley Railroad.

The Zealand area, for those not familiar with its history, was a
booming little logging community 100 years ago when notorious
timber baron James Everell Henry was sending work crews 11 miles
into the untamed Zealand and eastern Pemigewasset wilderness.

The village itself, situated about a half mile west of the present
day Zealand Road—halfway between Twin Mountain and Bretton
Woods—thrived for more than a dozen years in the 1880s and 1890s.
As many as 250 people lived in the village, which featured a sawmill,
a boarding house, a post office, a train depot, a company store, and
other structures.

As one drives along Route 302 now, it is nearly impossible to de-
tect any visible signs of this once bustling community. Yet just a few
yards from where automobiles now pass by on their way to and from
North Conway or Crawford Notch, the remains of this logging community are neatly camouflaged by roadside trees and vegetation.

As part of the archaeological tour of the Zealand area, workshop
participants first worked their way along the brushy slopes above the
south bank of the nearby Ammonoosuc River, carefully following
their way along an overgrown rail bed to the site of a former train
engine house and a nearby repair shop. Various tools and contrap-
tions left behind when the shops were abandoned nearly 100 years
ago littered the forest floor. Near what is believed to be the site of
the engine house, a 10-foot section of a metal smoke stack lies partially covered by the thick undergrowth.

Further up the actual Zealand River Valley, where Henry's wood-
fired steam engines worked their way into the forest as lumberjacks
cleared the region of its virgin spruce timber, the Forest Service
workers led the group along the USFS-maintained Trestle Trail,
which crosses the Zealand River at the same spot where a grand railroad trestle once stood (hence the name).

Following the grade of the railroad, Govatski stopped several
times to point out drill marks etched forever into ledges lining the
grade. And after 10 minutes of walking, the group headed off the

Forest Service worker Jim Hill, right, pinpoints on a map the former location of J. E. Henry's logging railroad in the Zealand Valley. With Hill is Twin Mountain resident Ray Chaput.

trail again to locate the remains of a half dozen or so riverside charcoal kilns, also operated by Henry while he was clearing the valley of its best timber.

Red bricks were scattered around the area of the kilns, while several 6 to 8-foot sections of rail lay partially embedded in the turf. Govatski explained that Henry's trains, loaded with four-foot lengths of hardwood timber, would access the kilns from a track situated above the rectangular brick structures. The wood would be unloaded directly into the kilns, and the finished product loaded onto a train using a railbed that was lower and closer to the river. The charcoal, pieces of which still could be found at the site, was eventually shipped to the major cities of southern New England.

The village of Zealand more or less disappeared from the map in 1904 after logging had all but ceased in the Zealand Valley. Henry and his logging trains were by then invading the East Branch country in Lincoln. Meanwhile a series of devastating forest fires had left the valley itself a "vast wasteland" according to writers of that era.

Walking along the riverbanks of the Ammonoosuc River, signs of the former logging community remain quite evident today. Two iron rails can be seen sticking oddly out of the river on its northern bank. Submerged timbers reveal the site of the dam just upstream from the sawmill. And in the thick, shrubby forest, no more than 50 feet from the highway, the last vestiges of the Zealand sawmill reside, its whereabouts unbeknownst to the thousands of travellers passing by the site each year.

It has been nearly 100 years since the demise of Zealand Village, and 97 years since the last of J. E. Henry's trains rumbled their way through the nearby valley, yet their presence is still remarkably evident to the trained eye and the willing explorer.

Let us hope, just as Forest Service personnel do, that the time bandits of the late 20th century do not undo 100 years of local history and heritage, and leave behind little for those forest users of the next century.

Logging Era Artifacts Deserve Rightful Place in Forest

July 10, 1996

The destructive practices of late-19th- and early-20th-century lumberjacks played a key role in the formation earlier this century of the White Mountain National Forest.

Denuding incredibly large tracts of land of their valuable timber, the lumber barons of this era in turn sparked efforts among conservationists to preserve what was left of the forested White Mountains region.

Evidence of the lumberjacks' intrusion into the most remote valleys and hillsides of the area still abounds today throughout the National Forest. In particular, the Pemigewasset Wilderness area serves as a forested museum to the days of logging railroads and backwoods lumber camps.

Ever since I began exploring the wilds of the White Mountain National Forest some 15 years ago, excursions into the Pemi have been among my most enjoyable. Forgetting for a moment that this area of the Whites contains some of the finest summits and most picturesque valleys in the region, what makes the Pemi so special are the many artifacts from the logging era that remain scattered throughout the woods, both near existing hiking trails and beyond.

Hikers heading into the Pemi along the Lincoln Woods and Wilderness Trails tramp along the railroad grade that for some 50 years was used by trains hauling timber out of the forest to mills like that operated for so many years in nearby Lincoln.

J. E. Henry, the most celebrated of the turn-of-the-century lumber barons, was the first to send lumberjacks deep into these woods a century ago. The Parker–Young Company, which bought out Henry's interests in 1917, continued logging and mill operations until the mid-1940s. By then, the U.S. Forest Service owned the land that once belonged to Henry and continued logging operations were being heavily discouraged.

Remnants of the logging era are clearly evident today to those tramping deep into the woods off the Kancamagus Highway. The former railroad grades, for instance, serve as footpaths into the wilderness, while the sites of several old logging camps are today homes to designated backcountry camping facilities.

Adventurous hikers wandering off trail in these woods will frequently stumble across rusting old logging tools left behind when the last lumbermen retreated from the woods. Iron rails, cookstoves, chains, and crosscut saws are a few of the items I've seen in my off-trail travels in the Pemi.

Perhaps the most conspicuous reminder of the logging era is the trailside wooden railroad trestle which spans Black Brook, some five miles in from the Kancamagus Highway. The trestle, believed to be the only logging railroad span still standing in the state, is some 80 or more years old. The last railroad use of the trestle probably occurred in 1946, when operations were under way to remove all the old iron rails from the former East Branch and Lincoln Railroad line.

While the Black Brook or Camp 16 Trestle, as it is known, has managed to survive the end of the logging era and occasional flash floods, its future is by no means guaranteed. In fact, there are some indications that the Forest Service would like to remove the structure, and other logging era artifacts, entirely from the forest.

The rationale behind the proposed dismantling of the trestle is that because it rests in a federally designated wilderness area, as few signs of human intrusion into the woods should be present. As far back as 1989, when the Forest Service finalized its Pemigewasset Wilderness Plan, the USFS was recommending the trestle's removal.

In recent months, the Forest Service has asked for public comment on the trestle's proposed removal and understandably the idea has not found favor with everyone. The Lincoln-based Upper Pemigewasset Historical Society, for one, has decided to push for the trestle's permanent preservation.

Quentin Boyle, the Historical Society's secretary, wrote in an April 30 letter to the Forest Service, "Rather than see this piece of our heritage destroyed, [the Historical Society] feels it should be kept in repair with appropriate signage."

A descendant of several former employees of Henry and the Parker–Young Company, Boyle stressed that the logging railroad era and the Black Brook trestle are "an integral part of the history of the town of Lincoln."

"This trestle is a vivid reminder of the days of J. E. Henry and the many miles of railroad that his company used to haul thousands of board feet of lumber out of the Lincoln woods," added Boyle.

In anticipation of its eventual removal, the Forest Service several years ago undertook a thorough study of the trestle, documenting its unique construction and its history. The study was conducted for the Forest Service by former Plymouth State College history professor William Taylor.

According to Forest Service personnel, a team of USFS workers will soon examine the various alternatives for the bridge, taking into consideration its permanent preservation and its eventual dismantling. Later an Environmental Assessment will be prepared, and sometime in the next year or two, a final solution for the trestle will be implemented.

While it is understandable that safety issues tied to the trestle are a concern to the Forest Service, since the aging trestle lies close by several much traveled hiking trails, it is harder to buy into the notion that leaving the trestle standing threatens the "wilderness" character of the Pemi.

The Pemi, by virtue of its permanent place in local logging annals, will never be a pristine wilderness area. The very fact that most of the trails snaking through this vast woodland use either old railroad grades or logging roads is proof positive that man once heavily encroached upon this region of the Whites.

It has been intimated to me that removal of the railroad trestle would likely be just the beginning of an all-out effort to remove other logging era artifacts from the Pemi. There is apparently federal money available for such a "cleansing" of the wilderness, and with money hard to come by these days, the Forest Service would welcome the extra funds with open arms, regardless of the consequences of the operation.

There is certainly a need for pure wilderness areas in the White Mountains, places where backcountry travelers can escape mankind's civilized annoyances and enjoy a bit of solitude. But memorable wilderness experiences may also be had in places like the present-day Pemi.

This is a special area of the White Mountain National Forest where pieces of yesteryear serve as permanent reminders of where we were a century ago, and just how far we've come since then. That is what makes the Pemi the treasure trove that it is today. Looting this treasure chest would serve no useful purpose.

Language Barrier an Issue
in Hiker Death

January 24, 1996

In recent years, high profile accidents on Mount Washington and along the Presidential Range have provided New Englanders with ample warning of the dangers of winter hiking and climbing.

The deadly winter and spring of 1993–94, when five persons lost their lives on the region's most famous mountain range, prompted popular Dublin, N.H.-based *Yankee* magazine to produce a lengthy cover story on New England's "Killer Mountain."

Certainly the major daily newspapers of the region also ran their share of stories on these mountain tragedies. The fact that the *Boston Globe* had a writer and photographer on top of Mount Washington when one of the most publicized of these deaths occurred did nothing, of course, to down play the seriousness of the incident.

While it can be surmised that all these stories have succeeded in making the public more aware of the dangers of winter mountain climbing, an event earlier this month on the southeastern slopes of New England's highest mountain reveals that much more public education needs to be done to ensure additional lives are not foolishly wasted in the cold and snow of the Presidentials.

On January 5, nineteen-year-old Quebec climber Alexandre Cassan was added to the growing list of mountain victims as he was buried alive by an avalanche near the recently closed Lion Head Winter Trail. Cassan, an experienced hiker with apparently limited winter mountaineering skills, was hiking in a party of four French Canadian climbers. Two in the party escaped the avalanche without injury, while one sustained multiple shoulder, leg and rib injuries. The other—that being Cassan—never made it off the mountain alive.

The perils of climbing Mount Washington are well documented. As the *Yankee* magazine story detailed last February, the death toll is climbing toward 120 persons, and many of those victims perished in cold or snow-related mishaps.

On the day that Cassan and his Quebec companions were attempting to summit the icy, snow-packed crown of Mount Washington, conditions were about as inhospitable as they can get.

On the mountaintop, 4,300 feet above the Appalachian Mountain Club's Pinkham Notch Visitor Center, temperatures were some 30 degrees below zero and winds were gusting in excess of 100 miles per hour. By all accounts, it was a nasty day on the mountain. It was a day in which only the foolhardy or the ignorant would dare challenge the peak and the elements.

Early in the morning of the accident, as is the case every day from December to June, U.S. Forest Service snow rangers Brad Ray and Chris Joosen were among the first humans to explore the lower reaches of the mountain. Their job, at least during the months when there is snow on the mountain, is to check the various ravines and trails to determine snow conditions.

Like everywhere else in New England, snow had been piling up on Mount Washington for the past two months. Just a day or two earlier, in fact, up to a foot of new snow had fallen. This snow, combined with other weather factors (temperature and wind included), caused the snow rangers to issue high avalanche danger warnings for both the Tuckerman Ravine and Huntington Ravine areas.

The Quebec hikers, who arrived at Pinkham Notch separately, but wound up teaming together for the climb, chose to take on the mountain despite the inherent avalanche dangers and inclement weather. By the time they departed from the base area, at around 10 a.m., avalanche warning signs had been posted for several hours, both at Pinkham and at several locations along the hiking trail to Tuckerman Ravine.

An AMC worker stationed at the base of Tuckerman Ravine was also telling climbers (including the four Canadians) that travel above treeline was inadvisable, and that any thoughts of attempting a summit climb should be dismissed.

The Canadians forged onward and upward, though, and eventually made their way onto the old Lion Head winter trail. This trail, which climbs steeply up Washington's southeast slope, has long been the most popular winter route up the mountain, but Forest Service officials just two months earlier decided to close the trail permanently due to potential avalanche dangers caused by a late fall landslide along a portion of the winter route.

Ignoring signs saying the Lion Head route was now off limits, the hikers started out on the trail, quickly lost their way, and very soon found themselves attempting to traverse a snow slope known for its avalanche potential. Whether the hikers themselves inadvertently started the snow slide, or whether they just happened to be in its path when it came sliding down the mountain is unknown. What is certain is that Cassan was quickly buried under the torrent of snow. When he was found about an hour later, only one of his hands was protruding above the snowpack.

Victim of Circumstances or Poor Judgment?

In the days immediately following the mountain tragedy, speculation centered on whether or not the French Canadian hiking party was a victim of poor judgment, poor luck, or a serious language barrier.

Certainly poor judgment played a major factor in this incident, and perhaps poor luck was also partly to blame, especially if the climbers did indeed just happen to be in the wrong place when the avalanche let loose. But the language issue is the one that appears to have the most credence, for no one is certain if the Canadians really knew for sure what they were getting into.

Rebecca Oreskes, a public information specialist for the U.S. Forest Service, said recently that confusion on the part of the hikers may have been a contributing factor in the mountain accident. She noted that trail signs at the Pinkham Notch base area and along the trail are all in English, and thus may have been unintelligible to the French Canadians. The hikers' poor English-speaking skills also suggest that verbal warnings about the trails and weather may have been unintentionally forsaken.

"We are looking at better ways to reach and educate Canadians," said Oreskes. "Somehow we have to get through to people that there are inherent risks to climbing Mount Washington, not just in winter, but in all times of the year."

Brad Ray, the longtime Mount Washington snow ranger, said this month's tragedy, while unfortunate, comes as little surprise since hikers routinely challenge the mountain in the worst of times.

Ray feels the number of French Canadian climbers who are taking to the mountain in winter has increased significantly over the years. The disturbing part of that trend is that Canadians tend not to be as well prepared for the range as they should be. "The Canadians that come to the mountain aren't anywhere near as prepared, both equipment-wise and knowledge-wise, as Americans," said Ray. Too often, he said, he runs into Canadian trampers who really have no business being on the mountain.

"We can tell these people the risks they're taking, but we can't prevent them from doing what they want to do," said Ray. "It's frustrating, but until they are further educated about these mountains, these tragedies are going to occur."

In the most recent issue of *Appalachia*, the AMC's biannual journal, accidents section editor Eugene Daniell III of Concord critiques two incidents on the Presidential Range last winter in which groups of French Canadian climbers ran into serious, though not fatal problems. Daniell writes, "It might seem to be a coincidence that both groups came from the Montreal area, but in fact there have been several near misses on the Presidentials involving hikers from that area in recent years, and the common thread seems to be total ignorance of the basic requirements of equipment, experience, and the ordinary safety practices demanded for cold-weather travel on Mount Washington and the surrounding peaks."

Daniell goes on to surmise that high publicity incidents in recent winters have educated New England climbers on the inherent dangers of winter hiking on Mount Washington. "Apparently such is not the case in Montreal," writes Daniell, "for the several groups that have gotten into trouble in the recent past have approached the range as if a winter-conditions traverse were a pleasant, even mellow jaunt for the novice backpacker."

As AMC publicist Rob Burbank noted in an interview just after the most recent accident, "people getting into trouble in the mountains isn't anything new." That's why AMC has taken the lead in recent years in emphasizing mountain safety through various educational programs.

While admittedly a problem, Burbank said the French language issue is secondary to the issue of backcountry preparedness. "Backcountry travel in all seasons is a case of self-reliance. It's important for hikers to have the right information in their heads when they start out on the trail."

AMC is not blind to the language gap, however, and has made attempts to address the issue. Burbank noted AMC's summer "Information Volunteer" program—in which volunteer hikers pass on pertinent trail information at popular places throughout the Whites (like Hermit Lake Shelter near Tuckerman Ravine)—this past year included several French-speaking persons from Quebec.

"But realistically, getting more education out to our Quebec visitors will be a long process," said Burbank.

The production of bilingual trail signs, which is something Brad Ray would like to see happen, "would be a major task" for AMC or the Forest Service to undertake. Ray says he'll push for the Forest Service to have workers like himself take courses in the French language.

"Somehow," said Ray, "we have to find a way to communicate better with the Canadians."

Backcountry Cellular Phones: Help or Hindrance?

March 13, 1997

A few years back, the Appalachian Mountain Club, U.S. Forest Service, New Hampshire Fish and Game Department and several other outdoors related agencies and groups put together a neat wallet-sized info card listing what hikers should take into the backcountry during both the warm and cold weather months.

The card lists many predictable items such as hiking boots, water bottles, first aid gear and a guidebook. Some frequently overlooked articles such as a space blanket, a trash bag and sun lotion are also included. For an item that measures just 3¾ inches by 2¼ inches, the card is pretty comprehensive and extremely informative.

To some hikers in this age of advanced technology, however, the plastic orange card may not be as up-to-date as they'd like to see. Its biggest omission, these hikers might argue, is an item that's use is becoming more common each day. These hikers have to be wondering why cellular phones aren't listed as recommended gear for White Mountains hikers.

As we have seen and heard in recent months, cellular phones and other similar communication devices (such as two-way radios, portable CB radios, etc.) are regularly making their way into hikers' backpacks and are being used frequently by those willing to lug them up a mountain or along some secluded backwoods trail.

The fact that cellular phones are being placed inside backpacks, alongside baggies of gorp and extra pairs of wool socks, is being met with mixed reviews from many in the hiking community. Although most see the potential of the phones as a lifesaver in certain instances, there's also a growing sentiment that they create more problems than they're worth, and that they can spoil or diminish one's backcountry experience.

From a safety standpoint, one can justify (I suppose) the presence of a phone or a radio in one's pack. In a dire emergency, where one is lost or injured, cellular phones can and have been used to call for help.

One question that arises, however, is whether the phones are a help, a hindrance, or merely an unnecessary tool?

Already in 1996 we have seen four hikers and climbers die on White Mountains slopes. In the case of three of the four victims, cellular phones or two-way radios were at the scene either when the victims died, or at the very least just a few minutes later. As Major Ron Alie of New Hampshire Fish and Game pointed out earlier this week, however, the mere presence of a cellular phone guarantees nothing when it comes to mountain mishaps. Two cases in point took place just in the past couple of weeks, both of which ended in mountain fatalities.

In the case of Nicholas Halpern, the 50-year-old Lincoln, Mass., attorney who froze to death after losing his way on Mount Eisenhower, the hiker had a cellular phone inside his pack, but for whatever reason, he never pulled it out to call for help, even when he was obviously off course.

In the case of ice climber Robert Vandel of Venice, Maine, who lost his life in a thousand foot fall down Pinnacle Gully, someone in the gully or at least at its base had a cellular phone with him. The phone, while useful in alerting authorities to the accident, did nothing to save Vandel, who was probably dead by the time the phone call was made to rescuers.

Major Alie, in a phone interview earlier this week, said Fish and Game is concerned that hikers carrying cell phones with them may unintentionally use them as a crutch in times of trouble.

"Too often we see or hear about hikers who have taken themselves beyond their limits," said Alie. "They think of the phones as something that can save them."

Citing an incident on Mount Flume earlier this year, in which winter campers called for help when one of the members of the hiking group became ill, Alie said if the campers had been more familiar with the operation of the gear they were carrying, no problems would have arisen in the first place. As things turned out, the supposed camping victim was able to walk out of the woods by himself, but not before rescuers had already assembled and were headed into the forest.

AMC spokesperson Rob Burbank said yesterday the proliferation of cell phones in the wild, while maybe not favored by all backcountry travelers, "is something we're learning to live with. We recognize that they are here, and are here to stay."

Burbank said the cell phones, in selected cases, can be useful tools in emergency situations. But they're no replacement for self-reliance in the backcountry.

"What you carry in your pack is important, but what you carry in your head is even more important," said Burbank. "The cell phones might help in times of trouble, but it's better that hikers know how to avoid running into problems in the first place."

Hikers, stressed Burbank, should rely less on technology and more on wilderness education to ensure a safe and enjoyable backcountry experience.

The other issue tied to the use of cellular phones is their perceived encroachment on the backwoods and wilderness areas of the mountains. For the hiker or backpacker who has walked into the woods to escape civilization and its many conveniences, few things are more irritating than to run across a camper who insists on bringing along his "boom box" stereo system, or a hiker who whips out his cellular phone and calls home to check in with family members.

In their 1993 book, *Wilderness Ethics: Preserving the Spirit of Wildness*, Laura and Guy Waterman touch extensively on this issue, and recall an incident a few years back when, after an eight-hour bushwhack through the wilds of the Pemi Wilderness, they emerged on the summit of remote Mount Carrigain where one member of their hiking party promptly took his phone (or radio) out of his pack and called his wife to tell her he'd be home a little later than planned.

"Right at that moment, what did the radio do?" ask the Watermans in their book. "Yes, it let his wife know we were safe and what time to expect us. But it did a lot more than that. It whispered to us that we'd never really been in wilderness all day."

I was a member of that hiking party, and what the Watermans say is true. After battling through the trailless woods all day, and not seeing another person during our eight hours of trekking, the phone call put everything in a different perspective. We weren't as far away from home as we thought.

"Are we making too much of a little harmless electronic gadget or two?" continued the Watermans. "What we're trying to say is that it's much more than a toy. The toy takes over any scene it's a part of. The mountains are not the place for communication with civilization. The spirit of wildness asks us to leave the radio at home."

Hiker Throws Caution
to the Wind

March 6, 1996

On a day when most winter hikers and climbers chose to stay indoors rather than challenge blizzardlike conditions in the mountains, 50-year-old Boston area attorney Nicholas Halpern took to the woods.

Even though prevailing weather conditions on New Hampshire's famed Presidential Range were totally inhospitable—with heavy snowfall and winds gusting to over 100 miles per hour—Halpern was determined to reach the summit of 4,760-foot Mount Eisenhower. It was a mountain he and a friend had tried to climb a week earlier, only to be rebuffed by a snowstorm. This time he set out on the Edmands Path all alone.

When Halpern failed to return to his Lincoln, Massachusetts home the night of February 25, his wife began making phone calls, trying to determine where her husband was. A state highway department crew, working the Crawford Notch area, looked for Halpern's Ford LTD Crown Victoria, but failed to find it. It would be early Monday morning before the vehicle would be discovered near the Appalachian Mountain Club's Crawford Notch Hostel. By then, in all likelihood, Halpern was dead.

The discovery of Halpern's frozen, lifeless body late last Tuesday afternoon tragically brings to the forefront once again the risks winter hikers take while in their pursuit of a White Mountains summit. Like that of the Canadian hiker killed earlier this year in an avalanche on a closed mountain trail, Halpern's death could have been avoided. Common sense could have and should have prevailed.

"The biggest mistake he made was getting out of his car that day," said New Hampshire Fish and Game Department's Lt. Eric Stohl, who coordinated last week's two-day search for Halpern. "But I guess he was pretty determined to climb the mountain in winter. Nothing was going to stop him."

Without signing in at the AMC hostel—where posted signs warned of 125 mph winds on nearby Mount Washington—Halpern hoofed his way a couple miles up the closed Mount Clinton Road and began his ascent along the 90-year-old Edmands Path. As he was alone, and the only person to use that trail on this nasty midwinter day, no one can say for sure if he actually made it to Eisenhower's domelike, exposed summit.

What can be ascertained, though, is that Halpern never made it back down off the mountain, at least not alive. Instead, two Androscoggin Valley Search and Rescue (AVSAR) members would stumble across his body—perched on a rock alongside remote Mt. Pleasant Brook—more than 48 hours after his ill-fated trek had begun.

As best as can be determined, Halpern was able to make his way well up the Edmands Path, probably to the point where it reaches treeline, and maybe even beyond. While Fish and Game authorities, including Stohl and Capt. Ron Alie, insist there is no reason to believe Halpern summitted the mountain, some AVSAR rescuers disagree, and they firmly believe the hiker's ill-advised trek to the summit contributed to his untimely death.

Veteran AVSAR member Mike Pelchat, who's been hauling bodies off these mountains for years, surmised earlier this week that Halpern was able to reach the summit, and that it was during the early part of his descent that the hiker either lost his way on the upper reaches of the trail, or simply stumbled into the narrow drainage area of Mt. Pleasant Brook after being overcome by the onset of hypothermia.

Pelchat said he's convinced that faint, windswept snowshoe tracks discovered by rescuers in the col between Mounts Eisenhower and Franklin were those of Halpern, and that if he was able to get that far, he probably also went the additional four-tenths of a mile to the summit.

"If he did try for the summit, that sealed his fate," said Pelchat. "He was as close to being in a blizzard as you can get. Hypothermia probably hit him so fast, he didn't realize how serious things had become."

Jeff Tirey of Lancaster, another AVSAR member and a former weather observer atop Mount Washington, said Monday most people underestimate the power of high winds. "They don't have a concept of what high winds are really like, or what they can do to a person's body." If Halpern did venture above treeline and attempt the summit climb, "then by the time he started back down, he'd have been very beat up by the winds. He would have been so hypothermic at that point, he probably wasn't capable of thinking straight and that made it all the easier to lose the trail," said Tirey.

Two AVSAR rescuers came across Halpern's snow tracks high up on the trail, near where the Edmands Path traverses the northwest side of the mountain just below the treeline. The tracks led steeply downward into the narrow, V-shaped drainage area of Mt. Pleasant Brook.

"It was one hell of a place to get down into," said AVSAR member Paul Cormier of Twin Mountain, one of several persons to take part in the grueling Tuesday night retrieval of Halpern's body.

Cormier, along with Pelchat, Stohl and Alie, said Halpern did the right thing (once he got lost) by trying to get off the mountain via the brook bed. "At some point he probably panicked, and thought to himself that getting to a stream was the only way out," said Cormier.

By that juncture, however, the hypothermia was no doubt beginning to severely limit his capacity to think and react coherently.

"His tracks along the brook tell me he was in pretty bad shape," said Pelchat.

"He was walking in the water in places that he shouldn't have been," concurred Fish and Game's Stohl, "then he evidently ran out of steam."

Less than a half mile from the trail that would have brought him back to Mount Clinton Road, Halpern's body simply gave out on him and when he sat on a rock, his feet still dangling in the icy cold mountain stream, the beginning of the end was at hand. By then he had lost his mittens or gloves somewhere along the way, and one of his snowshoes had disappeared. It was only a matter of time before his body would quit for good.

Stohl said it's fairly obvious that Halpern's hypothermic condition prevented him from taking rational measures to save himself. His backpack, which contained a couple of uneaten sandwiches, a compass, and a cellular telephone, looked as though it had never been disturbed.

Of the cellular phone, which Halpern could have used to call for help, Tirey speculates the hypothermic hiker never even thought to pull it out of his pack. "By the time he needed to use it, it was probably too late to save him anyway."

Pelchat added that although Halpern had a decent amount of foul weather gear with him, he wasn't wearing enough to protect himself from the ravaging winds of the ridgeline. "He was dressed like someone who was going to hike fast and hard," said Pelchat.

Halpern's best, warmest piece of clothing—a down-like parka—never left the back seat of his car. "When I saw that," said Pelchat, "I figured this guy was in trouble."

Should Halpern, under the prevailing conditions, have ventured into the mountains on his solo hike? That's a question everyone keeps asking, and most in the hiking community agree that under the circumstances, caution was literally thrown to the wind.

"We talked to some people who hiked up the Crawford Path to Mount Clinton that same day, and they said they turned around when they reached treeline because the conditions were so poor," said one rescuer.

If only such wisdom had been employed by Halpern, who was hiking barely two miles away on the neighboring Mount Eisenhower. If it had, he'd still be alive today, planning for the next winter hike that will now never be.

Permit Renewal Dogging AMC

July 12, 1995

The Appalachian Mountain Club's chain of backcountry huts, which for more than a century have accommodated visitors and hikers in the White Mountains, are under intense scrutiny in 1995 as AMC seeks to renew its permit to operate the eight hostels on National Forest land.

The huts, stretched out over a 56-mile section of the Appalachian Trail, include Lonesome Lake Hut in Franconia Notch, Lakes of the Clouds Hut on the southwest shoulder of Mount Washington, and Madison Spring Hut, the first of the structures built by AMC back in 1888.

AMC's existing 30-year permit to operate the huts on White Mountain National Forest land expires in October, and the permit renewal process promises to be a rocky one for the Boston-based organization. In recent months, critics of AMC have been outspoken in their comments about the huts and the way AMC does its business in the Whites. In fact, the call has gone out in some circles for AMC to phase out at least half of its huts.

Critics of AMC accuse the organization of using the money it makes from its White Mountains operation—i.e. the huts—to fund its research and educational programs, along with its environmental lobbying efforts. The fact that AMC has a waiver from the Forest Service and does not pay a cent to operate its facilities on National Forest land further muddies the water as far as the club's permit renewal is concerned.

Hardline critics of AMC—and there are a growing number of them in northern New Hampshire—say the club has lost touch with

The Appalachian Mountain Club's Lakes of the Clouds hut is one of eight back-country hostels operated by AMC throughout the White Mountains.

the people of the region and that AMC's lobbying efforts too often run counter to the wishes of North Country residents.

AMC officials admit they made a mistake two years ago when they aligned themselves with several other environmental groups in opposing the relicensing of dams on the Androscoggin River—dams which are vital to the operation of the paper mills of Berlin.

The fallout from that experience has left its mark on AMC, and now almost every aspect of the club's operations has come under the gun; from people like State Senator Fred King of Colebrook, Executive Councilor Ray Burton of Bath, the Coös County Commissioners and former AMC member Robert Kruszyna of Randolph, whose hard-hitting position paper on the permitting process was published recently in a Berlin daily newspaper.

Among other things, Kruszyna charges that AMC is "a large, rich, monopolistic organization, which has been doing pretty much what it wants on public land for the past 100 years."

He said the proliferation of AMC's White Mountains operations—including the huts, its backwoods shelters, and its Pinkham Notch Visitor Center—have "effectively tamed the wilderness that the forest may once have been." By successfully drawing hikers to its huts, AMC is defeating its self-avowed purpose of being a responsible conservation organization, he argues. "No amount of well-meaning education . . . prevents the environmental destruction" which occurs when large numbers of people tramp on fragile alpine areas such as are found near AMC's Lakes of the Clouds Hut or Greenleaf Hut on Mount Lafayette.

AMC officials, naturally, defend their operations, saying that money from their backcountry operation maintains and staffs the buildings as well as the programs, research and information services the club provides.

In the July issue of the club's membership magazine, *AMC Outdoors*, Executive Director Andrew J. Falender and club President Samual F. Pryor III dispute the claims that the club's WMNF operations are a "cash cow" for the club.

"We don't make a profit in the White Mountain National Forest. In fact, we spend $765,000 more there a year than we bring in— money that is made up through membership dues, contributions, endowment income, grants, and other revenues."

According to a recent story in the *Boston Sunday Globe*, AMC had $3.4 million in revenues last year from its White Mountains operations, including $1.58 million from the huts.

It's no secret that AMC uses some of its White Mountains revenue for expenses unrelated to the operation of the huts. Some of this money is diverted toward education and research programs, while some goes towards search and rescue efforts and trail maintenance.

Technically, at least under strict interpretation of the existing permit, those monies should not be counted against the AMC White Mountains revenues, and if that were the case, AMC would probably be showing a profit on its hut system. Of course the federal permit does not allow for the club to make a profit on the huts, thus making for more fodder for AMC critics.

In defense of AMC, it should be pointed out that the club, now 65,000 members strong, provides many services that would otherwise be unavailable in the National Forest. Without question AMC offers services that the Forest Service can't possibly offer in these times of tight budgets, thus their presence is appreciated in many respects.

Certainly AMC and the Forest Service have a long and unique relationship; a partnership that goes all the way back to 1911, when the White Mountain National Forest was created. The question critics like Kruszyna are asking now is whether or not it is finally time for there to be some distance placed between AMC and the USFS.

"That the AMC effectively controls recreation on the White Mountain National Forest is not solely its own doing. It is merely behaving like any other business, expanding, pushing, grasping at opportunities to have a bigger piece of the pie," writes Kruszyna. "That it has been altogether too successful can be laid at the doorstep of the Forest Service, which has, to a large extent, abdicated to the AMC its responsibility in the recreational sector."

It will be several months, at minimum, before the permit process plays itself out. It would surprise no one, however, if the process drags into 1996, and perhaps beyond. In the meantime, hikers will continue to shell out as much as $62 a night to stay in one of the AMC huts, and critics will continue to call into question the motives and modus operandi of the nation's oldest conservation organization.

AMC Has Long Been
a Good Neighbor

November 8, 1997

Early last week the U.S. Forest Service extended for a year the special use permit that allows the Appalachian Mountain Club to operate its backcountry huts and facilities on White Mountain National Forest land.

By granting the extension, the Forest Service has given itself an extra 12 months to decide what to do about the huts, which despite their longtime presence in the Whites, have recently become the central focus of anti-AMC sentiment.

As has been chronicled in this space before, the AMC has been placed on the defensive amidst charges that its huts, and revenue they bring in, are being used to advocate environmental measures that are sometimes contrary to that of the economic well-being of North Country residents.

As AMC goes through the process of obtaining a new long-term permit from the Forest Service, you can be assured that every aspect of the group's operations will be carefully scrutinized and analyzed.

AMC's huts, of course, have been around for more than a century. The Boston-based organization, the nation's oldest conservation group, built its first high mountain refuge back in 1888, in the col between Mount Adams and Mount Madison. In the intervening years, AMC also established high huts from one end of the mountains to the other. Together, these eight mountain huts (combined with AMC's roadside Pinkham Notch Camp) allow for an easy traverse of the Appalachian Trail through the Whites, as each hostel is approximately a day's hike apart.

The huts, while a significant part of the heritage of the WMNF, are not now and never have been favorites of the entire hiking public. Over the years the call has gone out on more than one occasion to have the huts boarded up and/or removed.

Citing the sanctity of the wilderness, the environmental impact of the hut operations, and AMC's hut fee schedule, oppositionists have said for years the huts aren't really needed. While convincing arguments can certainly be made about the negative impact the huts have on the forest, AMC itself has proven time and again to be a responsible mountain neighbor.

Since its formation in 1876, AMC has done more to promote and preserve the White Hills than any other singular entity, excluding perhaps the Forest Service. Early AMC members, for instance, first explored many of the region's highest peaks and helped establish trails to dozens of summits all across the region. As hiking gained popularity with the masses, it was AMC that established emergency refuges atop the mountains to aid trampers suddenly caught by inhospitable weather.

In the infant days of skiing, AMC was also a major promoter of that sport, annually hosting or taking part in races such as the American Inferno at Tuckerman Ravine.

The AMC of the latter 20th century maintains an even more active role in the White Mountains, and it is hard to imagine life in these hills without them. A quick overview of AMC reveals that the organization:

- Routinely offers workshops focusing on outdoors skills and safety, and natural history and conservation;
- Provides training and oversight to more than 200 naturalists, who throughout the year provide free interpretive programs to visitors throughout the Forest;
- Sees its personnel provide assistance in 70–100 search and rescue missions annually, many of them under weather conditions far from ideal;
- Maintains in excess of 300 miles of WMNF trails, with paid professionals and other volunteers contributing 30,000 hours of labor each year;
- Conducts valuable scientific research, concentrating its efforts primarily on plant ecology, air quality, and water resources protection.

AMC's backcountry facilities, which besides the huts include shelters and established campsites, serve an estimated 150,000 persons in the course of a year. Less than half of these persons are actually overnight users. A majority are just passersby, many of whom will stop just long enough to use a toilet facility or perhaps refill their canteens with cool, clean water.

AMC's Pinkham Notch Visitor Center on Route 16 sees another quarter million people pass through its doors annually. Again, a relatively small percentage are overnight guests. Most are either backpackers, tourists, or perhaps workshop attendees.

In 1994, AMC claims it lost money on its White Mountains operations, with expenses exceeding revenues by some $765,000. In response to complaints that its hut rates are out of reach to a majority of potential North Country users, AMC officials note that only seven percent of all AMC lodging guests last year paid the maximum $62 a night charge, which is levied during the peak months of the summer. In fact, AMC says 40 percent of the club's 77,791 lodging overnights cost the user $15 or less in 1994.

"The AMC huts are more than B and B's with a view," is how AMC's Rob Burbank put it earlier this year. He said the huts play a crucial role as high country education centers. They provide shelter from the elements, provide a convenient base for backcountry search and rescue efforts, and aid in the management of "high use" areas within the WMNF.

The economic impact of the huts and related AMC facilities is also worthy of note said Burbank. He said the club's White Mountains payroll exceeds $1.2 million each year, while the club pays into state coffers well over $100,000 annually in rooms and meals tax revenue.

What AMC has gone through in the past year, and what it is certainly bound to go through over the next 12 months, has and will continue to have an effect on how AMC does business from now on. Reach-out efforts have been nearly nonstop since last spring. They will continue, obviously, until the huts issue is resolved.

For now, let's just hope lots of good comes out of the ensuing high huts discussions, and that AMC, long a responsible member of the White Mountains community, emerges a year from now an even stronger, more reliable neighbor.

Peak to Peak

Mount Hale:
A Peak with an Interesting Past

August 30, 1995

A recent visit to the summit of 4,054-foot Mount Hale got me thinking about this mountain's interesting past. Like many of our high summits, this peak has quite a story behind it.

Situated just outside of Twin Mountain village, Mount Hale is the highest peak in what is commonly known as the Little River range. As seen from Twin Mountain village, the summit is frequently mistaken for one of the Twin Mountains (North or South Twin), for which the village is named. In actuality, only North Twin Mountain is seen from the village as one travels along U.S. Route 302.

The mountain is named for Rev. Edward Everett Hale (1822–1909), a Boston Congregational minister, author of the classic American short story "A Man Without a Country," and a mountain enthusiast who apparently took to the trailless woods frequently with onetime state geologist Dr. Charles T. Jackson.

As Mount Hale's summit was completely wooded, few mountain climbers took the time to explore its heights in the 19th century. Guy and Laura Waterman, in their book *Forest and Crag*, do mention that Eugene B. Cook, described as "one of the most indefatigable explorers of the 1870s and 1880s" sought out its summit during one of his many White Mountains explorations. For the most part, though, Mount Hale was unfamiliar territory.

Early hiking guidebooks of the region give short shrift to the mountain, and for good reason. In the aftermath of J. E. Henry's devastating logging excursions into the nearby Zealand Valley, and a series of widespread forest fires, much of the mountain was burned over.

The first Appalachian Mountain Club guidebook, published in 1907, recalls Mount Hale as being a "fine wooded peak" back in 1891. Sixteen years later, however, it is described as a "desolate, burned wilderness."

As horrific as the turn-of-the-century fires may have been, they did have one redeeming value. They left the summit practically free of trees, thus opening up a nice panoramic view of the surrounding Little River and Zealand Valley country.

No doubt inspired by its "unobstructed" view, trailbuilders eventually constructed a trail to Hale's summit in the mid-1920s. The first route to appear in print was described in the 1928 AMC Guide. Curiously, though, a route to the summit was shown on AMC maps previous to this, in the 1925 edition!

The first route to the mountaintop followed an old logging road which branched off the long abandoned Twin Range Trail along the Little River. In 1928, the path to the summit from this area was greatly improved with the construction of a tractor road, which was needed to haul material to the summit for construction of a new steel fire lookout tower.

The tractor road, which was 6 to 10 feet wide, zigzagged up the mountain's western slopes and can still be followed today by those who know where to find its valley origin. The road was used not just in summer, but also by winter sporting enthusiasts. Several editions of the AMC guide touted the road as being "an excellent ski run" for those with intermediate skiing skills.

Within a decade or so after the first trail up the mountain was built, Mount Hale was crowded with footpaths. By 1936, four routes to the summit—one from each direction òn the compass—were established, including the two trails (Lend-A-Hand and Hale Brook) that still remain.

The Lend-A-Hand Trail, which leads in 2.5 miles from AMC's Zealand Falls Hut to the summit, was constructed in 1934. At around the same time, the Hale Brook Trail from the Zealand Road was built, as was the Tuttle Brook Trail from Twin Mountain village.

The Tuttle Brook Trail, which left Twin Mountain from somewhere in the vicinity of the town's modern day recreation field, ascended the mountain from the north and linked up with the Mount Hale Trail (tractor road) about a half mile below the summit. Early guidebook descriptions of this trail, however, mistakenly said it connected with the Hale Brook Trail. The corrected version never appeared until the 1946 AMC Guide was issued—some 10 years and two editions after the trail was built.

Over time both the Mt. Hale Trail and Tuttle Brook Trail fell into disuse. The Mt. Hale Trail was abandoned by 1960 and Tuttle Brook Trail by 1963.

The steel summit fire tower, mentioned earlier, was operated by the U.S. Forest Service from 1929 to 1948. Its condition deteriorated rapidly once it was taken out of service. Although the steel frame remained on the mountaintop for several decades, all that remains now are the tower's concrete piers.

Mount Hale remains a popular hiking destination today, although visitors to its summit are no longer greeted with the "unobstructed" views of 60 years ago. Over the last decade, the trees atop the mountain have grown to the point where it is difficult to get a clear view into the valleys surrounding the mountain on three sides.

For years, the summit vista was known for its unique perspective of Zealand Notch and distant Carrigain Notch; the two of which line up neatly with one another. Even that view is hard to obtain these days, unless one is atop the mountain in winter and elevated by its cover of four or five feet of snow.

The Twin Range peaks, separated from Hale by the Little River, are the dominant mountains seen from the summit. The nearby Presidential Range, with 6,288-foot Mount Washington serving as its centerpiece, is also seen above the trees and to the east.

As Mount Hale is on the list of New Hampshire's 4,000-foot peaks, and is considered to be among the easiest to climb, hikers will no doubt continue to tramp to its summit. What hikers receive for their efforts, however, won't be what it was in years past.

Mount Cabot: Forgotten Peak of the North Country

Being removed as it is from the more frequently visited summits of the White Mountains, 4,170-foot Mount Cabot has never been a major attraction for visiting hikers.

Situated several miles east of Lancaster in the remote town of Kilkenny, Mount Cabot is not only the highest peak in the Pilot Range; it's also the highest 4,000-foot summit north of the Presidential Range and the east-to-west running U.S. Route 2.

The forest-covered mountain is rarely overrun by hikers, even on the clearest of summer days. Hikers, it seems, prefer the more accessible peaks, like those close to Interstate 93 or along the Route 302 or 16 corridors.

Were it not for the fact that Cabot's summit exceeds 4,000 feet, it's unlikely hiker traffic would be nearly as heavy as it is. Personal experiences have proven that the majority of trampers found on the summit are usually "peakbaggers," and the lone reason they've dared venture into this northern wilderness is to attain yet another peak on the New Hampshire Four Thousand Footer list.

Admittedly there are lots of peaks in the Whites that surpass Cabot in terms of beauty and summit vistas. Several veteran mountain climbers who've compiled view ratings of the highest White Mountains summits do, in fact, rate Cabot's at or very near the bottom of their charts.

Summit views notwithstanding, I have always found this North Country peak to be a friendly, hospitable place to visit, in almost any season of the year. My seven summit visits over the last 10 years confirm my fondness for this mountain.

Cabot's redeeming qualities may be hard for the average hiker to pick up on; especially those intent just on bagging the summit and then heading back down to their cars at the trailhead. A closer look at the peak, however, reveals a more interesting mountain than initially meets the eye.

For starters, I like heading up onto the heights of the Pilot Range knowing that my day on the trail won't include an endless parade of hikers either pushing their way up the mountain ahead of me or slogging their way up to my rear. There are no AMC huts in the area, so I don't have to deal with a steady stream of trampers. There are also no auto roads, or railroads, or well-tended, graded footpaths serving as open invitations for summit-seeking tourists.

In sharp contrast to the peaks of the Presidential Range, or the summits of Franconia Ridge, most of which can be seen from various outlooks along the way, Mount Cabot has a much wilder feel to it. Even though it can't technically be considered a true North Country mountain—an honor more appropriately bestowed on the mostly trailless peaks above Groveton and the village of Stark—it's near enough for one to get a feel for the much discussed, much threatened Northern Forest region of New England and upstate New York.

The trails that exist in this region of the White Mountain National Forest, and there aren't many of them, tend to be of a somewhat lesser quality than one would expect elsewhere in these hills. The Mount Cabot Trail, for instance, while quite decent along its upper reaches, will never be mistaken for the expertly built Edmands Path up Mount Eisenhower or the well-worn Bridle Path up to Greenleaf Hut and Mount Lafayette. It's a soggy, narrow footway through the woods for better than a mile, with few waterbars or bog bridges to keep the trail or one's feet from taking on water or mud.

On a recent hike up this trail I made the smart decision to wear my beat-up old hiking boots instead of my good-as-new, barely scuffed pair. The choice was a wise one as the trail resembled something more akin to the mucky Adirondacks of New York. If you've ever hiked up to some of New York's higher summits, you'll know just what I mean.

Cabot's much maligned summit view is deserving of its lackluster credentials, but there's more to the mountain than its uninviting top. I have always felt that the vista from Bunnell Rock, a ledgy outcropping 2.8 miles from the start, receives much less credit than it deserves. The view down into Bunnell Notch—the mountain pass separating Cabot's south slope from neighboring Terrace Mountain—is superb, as is the perspective on the north-facing slopes of Mounts Waumbek and Starr King.

Bunnell Rock also looks distantly upon many of the White's more famous western peaks (Lafayette, Cannon, and Kinsman among them). On a clear day, it's also possible to pick out the Green Mountain peaks of Killington and Pico, about 100 miles to the southwest.

The views improve even more from the site of the old firetower that for more than 40 years stood a third of a mile down from the true summit. In addition to offering unique perspectives on The Horn and Roger's Ledge to the northeast, the tower site amazingly allows one to pick out close to 40 summits of New Hampshire's much heralded Four Thousand Footers. Only a few peaks in the entire White Mountains region can back up that same claim.

Man's invasion of the mountaintop doesn't end with the firetower, which was demolished by the Forest Service 31 years ago. Just a few yards south of the tower stood a small cabin where the fire watchers spent their spring and summer evenings atop the peak. Although the tower is long gone, the cabin remains. It has long been maintained by a local Boy Scout troop and the Pinkerton Academy Outing Club. Open to overnight users on a first come, first serve basis, the rustic red structure even offers up a bit of history with its wall display of old summit photographs taken by local resident Warren Bartlett.

Due to space considerations, I will defer at this time from including the complicated road instructions to the Mount Cabot trailhead. It is far easier to refer those interested in hiking the peak to the *AMC White Mountain Guide*, long considered the "bible" for hiking in this neck of the north woods. The road directions are spelled out quite nicely in this book.

Of course it comes as no surprise that one must wade through 493 pages of text in the guidebook to find the Mount Cabot Trail description. That, however, is the way it is with this mountain. For even though it's tall, round, and quite conspicuous, Mount Cabot remains an afterthought in the minds of most White Mountains hikers.

The former firewarden's cabin atop Mount Cabot is now used as an overnight camping facility by hikers of all ages.

Fond Memories Abound
of Hikes to Mount Bondcliff

August 7, 1996

Nine years ago this week, and five years after I climbed my first White Mountains summit, I reached my 48th and final 4,000-foot New Hampshire peak.

Reaching the top of remote 4,265-foot Mount Bondcliff was no easy chore on that sunny, cool day in 1987. It's a 9.4-mile one-way trek to the summit from the Kancamagus Highway, and no matter how good a condition you're in, making the round-trip hike in a single day is a tiring ordeal.

If memory serves me correctly, my hiking companion for the day, Steve Smith, and I headed out onto the trail bright and early that brilliant Thursday morning. We cruised for five miles along what was then known as the Wilderness Trail, then spent the last 4.4 miles trudging uphill along the moderate grades of the Bondcliff Trail.

By 11:15 a.m. we were atop the craggy summit of Bondcliff, looking down upon the wooded East Branch and Franconia Brook valleys, and scanning skyward up to the neighboring peaks of Mount Bond and West Bond.

It was easy to see why the AMC hiking guidebook in my possession at the time said the outlook from Bondcliff and its range of summits "commands views that are unequalled" in the White Mountains, with barely a sign of mankind visible from the mountain's upper reaches.

It was partly by design, partly by accident, that I ended my quest to reach New Hampshire's 4,000-foot summits on top of Bondcliff. If the weather had been more cooperative a year earlier, when I set out on a three-day backpacking excursion that was to include a traverse of the three peaks of the Bond Range, the last peak left on the list would have been Mount Isolation, which Steve and I had scaled a few weeks prior to our Bondcliff hike.

My August 1986 trip to the Bonds was cut short by foul weather that included heavy rains, fall-like temperatures, and winds gusting to over 50 miles an hour. While daring to brave the elements to reach the more sheltered peaks of Bond and West Bond (from my camping spot at Guyot Shelter), I chose to bypass the planned climb to Bondcliff's exposed, windswept summit. Not knowing what to expect of the mountain, and having been forewarned by my *AMC White Mountain Guide* about the hazards of crossing over this peak in poor weather, I played it safe and opted to take on the mountain some other day.

Ultimately, as I got nearer and nearer to completing the list of peaks, the decision was made to make Bondcliff the final summit. It was also decided that I would only make the climb on the nicest of days, even if it meant waiting a few days, weeks, or even months to catch just the right combination of sun, wind and temperature.

Because of the circumstances surrounding my first ascent of Bondcliff, the mountain has remained dear to my hiking heart. And while my return trips have been few and far between, each has been special in some way.

For a period of four years, I managed to make it back to Bondcliff just about once a season, and to this day, these mountain adventures rank among my most cherished.

My second visit to Bondcliff took place in March 1989 when Steve, Roger Doucette of Whitefield, and I made a rare winter visit to the Bonds. Blessed with ideal late winter snow and weather conditions, our day-long 20-something mile hike featured visits to all three Bond summits and a memorable two to three-mile bushwhack hike from the summit of West Bond down to the Franconia Brook valley via the mountain's thickly wooded, snowy southwest ridge.

A few months later, in August, Steve and I organized and took part in the first ever fund-raising White Mountain CROP Walk hike to curb worldwide hunger. Our ambitious agenda, which included ascents of five 4,000-footers, covered more than 20 miles and was capped off by a late afternoon ascent of Bondcliff. Time constraints allowed us just a half-hour stay atop the peak, but it was 30 minutes that were well-invested as the view across the East Branch towards the peaks of the eastern Pemi Wilderness were indescribable.

My fourth (and last) visit to Bondcliff took place nearly six years ago as I took advantage of some unusually warm Columbus Day weekend weather to return to Guyot Shelter campsite for two nights out in the woods. The other motivating factor for this trip was the planned summit wedding of Pennsylvania trampers Howard Feist and Susan Wonsik. Attending the midday ceremony in the guise of a newspaper reporter, I also wound up serving as official wedding photographer for the event.

As I look back on my rare visits to this spectacular White Mountains summit, I can almost feel myself being tugged back in the direction of Bondcliff. Six years, I am being reminded, is too long to be away from a mountain that has had such a lasting impression on my hiking psyche.

Before the year is out, perhaps I will visit this mountaintop again. It's been 125 years since Bondcliff was first ascended by Warren Upham and an unnamed Dartmouth College student, both of whom were taking part in the monumental 1871 geological research expedition headed up by state geologist Charles Hitchcock. That's an anniversary worthy of a celebratory trip, just like my own milestone hike to Bondcliff on Aug. 6, 1987.

Mount Jackson: Unheralded, But Worthy of a Climb

August 2, 1995

Mount Jackson will never rival its Presidential Range sister peaks to the north. Its summit, at 4,052 feet above sea level, is some 2,000 feet lower in elevation than towering Mount Washington's, and its connecting ridgeline is absent of the rare alpine plants and flowers found elsewhere on this famous White Mountains range.

Mount Jackson also does not play host to the hordes of hikers that frequent Tuckerman Ravine or the Appalachian Mountain Club's Lakes of the Clouds Hut. Heck, it's not even named for someone who served in the Oval Office, even though it's a member peak of the Presidentials.

In spite of its unimpressive credentials, however, I have long found this peak to be among my favorites. Initially its status as a Four Thousand Footer was the drawing card; now it's the summit view and the moderate grade of the trail which attract me.

Situated along the southern reaches of this great range, between the higher peak of Mount Pierce and the lower peak of Mount Webster, Jackson's summit is the easiest to reach in the Presidentials. It is just 2.5 miles by trail to its conical, mostly open summit. Only the last 0.2 mile can be construed as steep.

As mentioned earlier, Mount Jackson's name belies the fact that it's a member of the Presidential Range. Unlike most other peaks within the range, this mountain is named for someone other than a former U.S. President. Instead, it is named for one time State Geologist Charles Thomas Jackson, one of the Granite State's most ambitious 19th-century scientists and explorers.

Botanist William Oakes, who first visited this peak in 1876, is

169

credited with christening the summit in Jackson's honor. There are conflicting stories as to exactly how this christening came about, but the commonly held belief is that Oakes sent a companion explorer of his to Jackson's summit and had him start a bonfire there to mark the official naming of the mountain.

For most of the 19th century, Mount Jackson was an infrequently visited mountain. Guidebook author Moses Sweetser, in describing the mountain, wrote, "The greater part of the summit is masked with trees, a circumstance which renders it of little interest to the lover of scenery."

He noted that the most popular route to its summit was from Mount Clinton (or Pierce), which had long been accessible by trail thanks to the efforts of the Crawford family. To get to Jackson, though, required a rugged bushwhack. "The transit is laborious, the way being frequently obstructed by thickets of dwarf spruce," wrote Sweetser.

In 1876, William Pickering, a noted astronomer of the times, also had little good to say about the mountain. After bushwhacking to the summit from nearby Mount Webster, he said Jackson's summit had a "most lonely appearance."

In this day and age of peakbagging, one would be hard pressed to describe the summit of Mount Jackson as still being lonely. It's nearness to Crawford Notch and Route 302, and its scant 1.7-mile distance from AMC's popular Mizpah Spring Hut, make it a popular destination with day hikers and backpackers.

The 2,160-mile Appalachian Trail also passes over its summit as it wends its way north from Georgia to Maine. In fact it is during this time of summer each year that northbound thru-hikers are just beginning to emerge onto the Presidential Range after four solid months of daily 15–20 mile treks.

Jackson's summit view, obscured partially by trees, is not nearly as spectacular as that from a summit like Mount Adams or Mount Eisenhower, but it's still a fine reward for the amount of effort put into its ascent. Certainly few mountaintops offer up as good a view to the south as does Jackson. The twisting valley of the Saco River provides the dramatic foreground for the most distant peaks seen in this direction from the summit. Mount Chocorua's pointed crest is the centerpiece landmark to the south. Rising up on either side of the Saco River valley are the lower summits of the Montalban Ridge

The view southwest from Mount Jackson's summit takes in the peaks of the Willey Range in nearby Crawford Notch.

to the east, and the higher summits of the Nancy–Bemis Ridge to the west.

From various spots atop the summit, far-reaching vistas are also afforded in all other directions. Mount Carrigain, the dominant peak of the Pemigewasset Wilderness, stands proud and tall to the southwest, while much nearer and a bit north of Carrigain are seen the summits of Mounts Willey, Field and Tom—the triple peaks forming the western wall of Crawford Notch.

To the north and east, of course, are the peaks of the southern Presidentials. Mount Clinton, with Mizpah Spring Hut tucked under its south-facing slope, gives way to Eisenhower, Franklin, Monroe and finally Mount Washington.

The easiest and most direct route to Jackson's summit is via the Jackson–Webster trail, which leaves Route 302 just a couple hundred yards north of the great cut at the top of Crawford Notch. With the exception of a few short, steep pitches (most notably the one approaching the summit), the trail up Mount Jackson ascends on a moderate grade.

The first 1.5 miles of the Webster–Jackson Trail pass close by several outstanding rock outcroppings high above Crawford Notch. The first, known as Elephant Head, is reached by a 0.2 mile side trail to the right, just a tenth of mile from the start of the hike.

At 0.6 mile, another side trail to the right leads up and then down to Bugle Cliff, a much higher ledge with superb views down into the Notch and also toward the site of the former Crawford House hotel.

For the next three-quarters of a mile, the trail ascends easily to a point where the Webster–Jackson Trail forks. Straight ahead in 1.1 miles is the 3,910-foot summit of Mount Webster. To the left is the mile-long route to Mount Jackson.

On the way up to Jackson, several areas of severe blowdown are passed. In places, trees lie like fallen matchsticks on either side of the trail. The way is rougher and more rocky the higher one gets, and just after passing by Tisdale Spring (signed) less than a quarter mile from the summit, the character of the terrain is such that a bit of careful rock scrambling is required.

In descending, hikers have several options to choose from. These include backtracking over the ascent route, taking the Webster Cliff Trail south to the summit of Mount Webster, or heading north along the Webster Cliff Trail to Mizpah Spring Hut, and then connecting onto the Crawford Path for the descent back to Route 302.

An Early Summer Trek
Up Mount Eisenhower

June 21, 1995

The month of June conjures up many memories for me as I look back on my 13 years of exploring the White Mountains. Most, of course, are pleasant ones, but there are a few that I would most certainly trade if one could possibly do so.

When I think of Junes past, I recall a 1984 trek to the northern Presidential Range peaks of Jefferson and Adams—a hike which left me as weary and sore as I have ever been, on any hike, in any month of the year. I also remember a 1986 solo backpacking venture along the Carter range, the first time I had ever attempted such an overnight trip without the guidance of more experienced, woods-wise companions.

In 1987, June found me making the long haul to appropriately named Mount Isolation as I closed in on completion of the New Hampshire Four Thousand Footer peakbagging list. And in June 1992 I climbed New England's highest peak, Mount Washington, attempting to retrace the footsteps of Darby Field, who 350 years earlier had become the first man to reach the top of the Rock Pile.

During this first month of summer, I have encountered clouds of black flies practically everywhere I've ever gone. I've marveled at the rare alpine plants growing along the highest, most exposed areas of the Presidential Range. I've also run into gangly moose, hailstorms, high-heeled tourists and a bear or two.

June is not my favorite month for hiking. September and October have it beat by a mile. Nonetheless, a quick glance at my personal hiking register shows I have beaten a path through the mountains of New Hampshire as often in June as in any month of the calendar year.

Because I have no love for the bloodsucking black flies which all too often have wreaked havoc with my early summer outdoor excursions, I try each year to choose trails and mountains where the bugs aren't likely to be so bothersome. Finding a spot where the wind blows consistently is the best preventive medicine when it comes to shaking off the little suckers.

The lofty peaks of the Presidential Range, naturally, come immediately to mind when one starts thinking or talking of wind. Rare is the day when a hiker doesn't encounter some type of breeze while exploring the exposed heights of the region's most celebrated mountain range. That's why I'm more likely to be found traipsing around the Presidentials this time of year than heading onto some completely forested mountain ridge.

For my first major trail excursion this June, I opted to tackle the heights of 4,761-foot Mount Eisenhower. The round, symmetrical done of this mountain is, as one 19th-century guidebook author wrote, "the most conspicuous" peak in the southern reaches of the Presidentials.

Situated approximately halfway along the Crawford Path between the height-of-land at Crawford Notch and grand Mount Washington, Mount Eisenhower is arguably the finest of the peaks along this portion of New Hampshire's most famous mountain range. As recent research appears to indicate, Eisenhower's summit was one of the first in the White Mountains to be climbed, though admittedly it was not the planned destination of its first visitors. Historians who buy into the theory that Darby Field's landmark 1642 ascent of Mount Washington was made along the same ridge that is now traversed by the Crawford Path accept the fact that Field and his indian companions passed over Eisenhower's summit prior to reaching the top of Mount Washington, some four miles or so distant.

Until 1820, the mountain was a nameless, but prominent hump along the ridge running south from Mount Washington. It was first dubbed Pleasant Mountain, but has also been known as Pleasant Dome and Dome Mountain. It was officially renamed Mount Eisenhower in 1972 in honor of Dwight D. Eisenhower, the nation's popular 34th President.

Mount Eisenhower lies along the ridgeline between Mount Pierce (or Clinton as some still call it) and Mount Franklin, and its most striking features include its massive, round shape—seen especially well from the Bretton Woods–Crawford Notch area—and its expansive, nearly flat summit area, some six acres in size.

Near the northeast base of the summit cone lies Red Pond, a small mountain tarn described by guidebook author Moses Sweetser as a "dull puddle of bad water." Red Pond is unique in that in times of heavy rain, it purportedly drains into both the Ammonoosuc and Saco River valleys. The pond gets its name from the red moss which is so prolific in the general vicinity of the mountain.

In his 1890 book, *The White Mountains, A Guide to Their Interpretation*, Julius Ward marveled at the vista afforded by Eisenhower's treeless summit. "The ridge from the peak of Jefferson to that of Washington looks like the wall of a fortress laid close to the sky, and the whole range might bid defiance to the armaments of the world."

Certainly the view from the summit towards Mount Washington is the most dominating vista, with the lesser peaks of the range—Mount Monroe and Mount Franklin—in the foreground below and to the right of the Rock Pile. Closer at hand, and directly below the mountain to the west lies the broad plain of the Bretton Woods area, dominated by the massive, red-roofed Mount Washington Hotel and its finely manicured grounds and golf course.

The Edmands Path off Mount Clinton Road, 2.3 miles from Route 302 at Crawford's, provides the most direct way to the summit and was the chosen route for my recent ascent. From the trailhead, it's a pleasant 2.9 mile walk to the junction of the Crawford Path, 0.4 mile north of the summit in the col between Eisenhower and Franklin. The way to the summit is via the Mount Eisenhower Loop, which meets back up with the Crawford Path a short distance south of Eisenhower's massive summit dome.

The grades along the Edmands Path are quite moderate and accommodating to a hiker's legs. Credit for this must go to the trail-building efforts of J. Rayner Edmands, who some 90 years ago constructed this path from the Bretton Woods area up onto the Presidential Range. His painstaking efforts are still evident along the middle and upper portions of the trail, despite the ravages of time, the mountain's severe weather, and the steady parade of hikers who have used this footway for close to a century now.

As one approaches the Crawford Path junction north of the summit, the trail emerges out of the scrub forest and above treeline, where winds tend to be brisk and chilling, even in the warmer months of the year. To reach the summit from the Crawford Path, the Mount Eisenhower Loop climbs steeply up the north slope of the peak, passing by (at least at this time of year) several species of rare alpine plants, of which hikers should be careful not to tread upon. You'll know you've reached the actual summit when you come across a large cairn (or pile of rocks) which marks the high point of the mountain.

Under windy conditions—which as I said in the beginning are usually welcome by hikers during black fly season—there are few places on the flat summit to escape what can often be a brutal, lashing breeze. About all one can do it hunker down on the lee side of the cairn, which usually provides a small measure of relief, even under the worst of conditions.

Considering the significant elevation gain attained by hikers (2,761 feet) utilizing the Edmands Path to get to the summit, the hike up Eisenhower is pretty mellow compared to that of other 4,000-foot summits in the Whites. You can usually anticipate a three-hour long ascent and a descent of perhaps two hours and change.

The Nature of Crawford Notch

August 21, 1996

Of all the areas I frequent in my travels through the woods and up to the summits of the White Mountains, none gives me more pleasure than the Crawford Notch region.

With its storied past, its remarkable scenic beauty, and its wide variety of terrain and natural features, Crawford Notch has something to offer to just about everyone.

My love affair with this famous mountain pass began 10 years ago when I enjoyed a five-month fling with the area as a state park worker. I had just relocated to the White Mountains after several years in busy southern New Hampshire and thoroughly enjoyed spending my eight-hour working days in the midst of the Notch, and not at a desk with a computer screen staring me in the face.

Unlike its sister mountain park, state-owned Franconia Notch, Crawford Notch has a wilder, more natural feeling to it. Its remote setting, being 10 miles or so from the nearest village of any measurable size, sets it apart from Franconia Notch, which is just a few minutes drive along the interstate highway from either busy Lincoln-Woodstock or from downtown Franconia.

Steep rocky slides, not wide ski slopes scar the higher peaks of Crawford Notch. There are also no aerial tramways, no modern visitor centers, and no fancy superhighways in Crawford Notch.

Of course Crawford Notch can't offer up anything like the venerable Franconia Notch rock profile, the Old Man of the Mountain. It does have the Elephant Head profile, though, which I suspect has been greeting visitor's to Crawford's probably as long as the Old Man has been welcoming tourists and the like to Franconia.

177

Crawford Notch, once known as the Notch of the White Mountains, also has plenty of character associated with it. Its namesake family made its mark on White Mountains history by establishing the first overnight guest houses for the infrequent travelers who had begun making visits to the White Mountains in the early years of the 19th century. The Crawfords were also responsible for constructing some of the earliest trails to the summit of grand Mount Washington, the highest peak in the Northeast.

The reestablishment of train service through Crawford Notch last fall, meanwhile, has sparked renewed interest in the fabled history of railroading through the area. A careful look back at the building of the railroad through the Notch some 125 years ago reveals how remarkable an achievement this was considering the resources construction crews had at their disposal in that time period.

It's the natural features of the Notch that are most attractive to me, though, and thanks to a vast network of trails in the immediate area, many of these features are easily accessible by foot.

The hike up to the summit of 2,804-foot Mount Willard is no doubt the most renowned hike in the Crawford Notch area. For relatively little effort, and less than a mile and a half of walking, one gains no better a perspective on the Notch than from atop Willard's summit cliffs. From this dramatic vantage point, the u-shaped floor of the Notch, carved out centuries ago by a glacier, is most noticeable, as are the great mountain ridges which form the eastern and western walls of the Notch itself.

Crawford Notch's network of hiking trails lead to many other unique natural areas. South of the Willey House site—scene of the much told Willey family tragedy of 1826—lie two of the White Mountains region's tallest and prettiest waterfalls: Ripley Falls and Arethusa Falls. Ripley Falls is but a 20-minute hike from Route 302, while 200-foot hike Arethusa Falls on Bemis Brook sits back nearly a mile and a half from the highway. Conveniently, both are interconnected by a trail that runs about three miles along the relatively flat ridge behind another of Crawford Notch's more notable landmarks, the precipitous Frankenstein Cliffs, which stand watch over the southern reaches of the state park.

The higher summits of the immediate area are accessed by several major trails. The 2,160-mile Appalachian Trail, which runs from Georgia to Maine, passes through the Notch and crosses Route 302

The lower slopes of Mounts Webster, Willard and Willey as seen from the Elephant Head profile in Crawford Notch.

about one mile south of the Willey House site (headquarters of Crawford Notch State Park). The Webster Cliff Trail, a link in the AT, ascends 3,910-foot Mount Webster from this point, and the walk along its ledgy ridge is one of the most spectacular, but unheralded hikes in all of New Hampshire.

Opposite Mount Webster, on the other side of the Notch, are the three 4,000-foot peaks of the Willey Range. A much used trail traverses the summits of Mounts Willey, Field and Tom. The section of trail up Willey's south face is among the toughest and steepest in the Whites and challenges even the fittest hiker.

The casual or occasional tramper is not left out when it comes to hiking about Crawford Notch. Certainly the short trek to Ripley Falls is suitable for most any hiker. The same may be said for the easy loop hike around picturesque Saco Lake at the head of the Notch, or the gentle walks along the Sam Willey and Pond Loop Trails across from the Willey House site near Willey Pond (or Reflection Pond as it is also known).

Yet another easy, but worthwhile short hike is the 0.3-mile walk to the top of the Elephant Head. From this unique vantage point are

The enduring splendor of Mount Willey and Crawford Notch are evident in this state publicity photo from the 1950s.

seen the waters of Saco Lake on the east side of Route 302 and the grounds of the former Crawford House above and slightly to the left of the lake. More distantly is also seen the red-roofed Mount Washington Hotel—the last of the grand hotels to grace the Bretton Woods–Crawford's area.

Elephant Head also provides a bird's eye view of the Conway Scenic Railroad train operation, which runs daily excursion trains in summer and fall from North Conway to the old train depot at the top of the Notch (and beyond to Fabyan's and Bretton Woods). The depot, meanwhile, serves as an invaluable hiker information center and is staffed by knowledgeable workers for the Appalachian Mountain Club.

Crawford Notch even provides spectacles of sorts to the passing motorist who has no time (or interest) to walk the region's hiking paths. Certainly the rugged splendor of the Notch is evident when one passes through the narrow stone "Gateway" at the height of land. Just a few hundred yards below the Gateway are the tumbling waters of the Flume and Silver Cascades, both seen on the left as the highway begins its steep descent to the floor of the Notch.

Having spent time in Crawford Notch four of the last five weekends, it's easy now for me to see why I fell for this area of the White Mountains 10 summers ago. It's a place with character, ruggedness, and accessibility—all features that add up to the grandest of the White Mountains notches.

Mountain Nuggets

Fifty Years of Change
on White Mountains Trails

July 24, 1996

From one year to the next, the vast network of hiking trails that snake their way through the White Mountains see few major changes. Except in rare instances when sections of trail are relocated, new trails are constructed, or man-made objects found along the way are dismantled or removed, what you see today is pretty much what you're apt to see tomorrow, or next year, or even four or five years down the road.

It is only over a much greater span of time—several decades, for instance—that significant alterations and changes are evident. Ongoing human encroachment into the forests and mountains is frequently to blame for what transpires. Weather is also a factor, as was quite evident nearly 60 years ago when the destructive Hurricane of 1938 forever changed the layout of trails in the region.

A look back at the Appalachian Mountain Club's 1946 edition of the *White Mountain Guide* provides a clear picture of the changes that have taken place on and along area trails in the last 50 years. In some instances, the reformation has been dramatic.

In 1946, for instance, trampers attempting a traverse of the southern Presidential Range did not have the luxury of coming upon one of the AMC's famed backcountry huts near what had long been known as Mizpah Spring. Instead, the area where today's Mizpah Spring Hut rests was apparently quite inhospitable to hikers, even though an overnight log shelter had been established at the site by AMC. The 1946 guide states, "Since the 1938 hurricane, the area around the shelter has been a scene of utter desolation."

It would be nearly 20 years later that AMC would build a new, modern backcountry facility at the site. The hut remains AMC's youngest member in the chain, being just 31 years of age.

Fifty years ago, hikers heading up to Mount Hale in the Little River area had twice as many routes to decide upon as they do today. In 1946, one could attack the summit from four different directions. Today the choices are limited to either the Hale Brook Trail off Zealand Road or the Lend-A-Hand Trail from Zealand Falls.

Both the Tuttle Brook Trail, which approached the summit from the north, and the Mt. Hale Trail which ascended from Little River to the west, were utilized by hikers back then. Although signs of the Tuttle Brook Trail no longer exist, the Mt. Hale Trail, which followed the course of the old fire road to the summit, may still be traversed if one is able to track down the start of the woods road as it climbs away from Little River, a short distance from the existing North Twin Trail.

Summer visitors to Mount Hale's summit in 1946 would also have been greeted at the top by the old steel fire tower which was operated by the U.S. Forest Service from 1929 to 1948. Today only the concrete piers which supported the structure are evident at the summit.

Fire towers were a regular sight atop many of the higher summits back in 1946. Mount Cabot in Lancaster, Mount Garfield in Bethlehem, Mount Osceola near Waterville Valley and Mount Carrigain near Livermore were among the mountains which were occupied by fire watchers at the time.

The guidebook description of the Carrigain Notch Trail told of the telephone line to the summit running close by certain segments of the path. The same was true of the phone line to Mount Garfield along its namesake trail. Small sections of the line may actually be seen today along this route, but only the most observant hiker will notice them lying in the thick brush alongside the footpath.

In 1946, just one major ski trail scarred the otherwise wooded west-facing slopes of Wildcat Mountain. Two ski trails also existed on Mount Tecumseh in Waterville Valley, while the Rosebrook Range was traversed by several old hiking trails; not the conglomeration of ski runs which today constitute Bretton Woods Ski Area. Loon Mountain was also a destination for hikers, and not a carload of downcountry ski enthusiasts.

In the Pemigewasset Wilderness, and particularly in the Cedar

Brook drainage area, logging operations were about to cease in 1946. Mount Hancock, now among the more accessible high peaks in the Pemi, was seldom visited 50 years ago as no trails existed to its summit. "Nearly the whole mountain has been logged and several slides scar its side," said the AMC Guide. "At best . . . the ascent is a stunt to be undertaken only by strong climbers with a knowledge of woodcraft who should be prepared to camp overnight."

Access to the Hancocks was limited also because the Kancamagus Highway had yet to be completed. While it had been extended from Lincoln village to the North Fork of the Hancock Branch (near today's Greeley Ponds trailhead lot), the distance and rough terrain obviously discouraged hikers from attempting to reach either of the mountain's two wooded summits.

The practice of "peakbagging" summits in the Whites was also a relatively unknown phenomenon five decades ago. Since hikers weren't beating the bushes to reach the tops of New Hampshire's 4,000-foot summits, mountains like Galehead and Owl's Head were unfamiliar to most trampers. Galehead, in fact, didn't even warrant a listing on the Franconia area map included in the guidebook. Only its elevation, then believed to be 3,948-foot, shows up between the map's brown-colored contour lines.

Certainly most trails in the White Mountains have undergone few changes in 50 years, while many of the perils that exist today did so as well back then. The editors of the guide made it quite clear that Mount Washington was as notorious then as it is now. As the guidebook noted, "The appalling and needless loss of life on this mountain has been due largely to the failure of robust trampers to realize that wintry storms of incredible violence occur at times even during the summer months. Don't attempt Mount Washington if you have a 'weak heart' or are in any way below par."

Which goes to show, I suppose, that the more things change, the more they also stay the same.

Guidebooks Continue
to Lead the Way

August 16, 1995

A hiker's backpack is generally filled with an assortment of items ranging from water bottles and bandages to t-shirts and insect repellant.

To ensure a safe and comfortable hiking experience, these items, and many others are a necessity, not a luxury.

Of all the things I stuff into my assortment of backpacks—be it my small day-hiking pack or my voluminous overnight pack—no single item has ever gotten more use than my guidebook.

Both on the trail and in the comfort of my living room, I have spent hours scanning the pages of my collection of guidebooks. They have helped shape very nearly every mountain adventure of mine, leading me to the summits of Mount Lafayette and North Twin Mountain, and into the lonely recesses of wild Carrigain Notch and silent Tunnel Ravine.

In these parts, the revered *AMC White Mountain Guide* is the guidebook of choice among trampers. Long known as the White Mountains "hiker's bible," this book is in its 25th edition and the current 638-page volume bears little resemblance to the comparatively small, 200-page green buckram leather edition that first appeared in 1907.

The AMC Guide is updated about every five years and covers hiking trails not just in the northern reaches of the state, but elsewhere as well. Certainly the 150 pages devoted to Mount Washington and the Presidential Range peaks are evidence of its primary focus. But one can also find trail information about the Monadnock Region of southwestern New Hampshire, the beautiful Lakes Region in the central part of the state, and the Connecticut River Valley.

Any visit to a bookstore will reveal there is no shortage of literature devoted to the trails of the region. Besides the all encompassing AMC Guide, there are also guidebooks to area waterfalls and lakes and ponds, guidebooks geared towards family hikes, and guidebooks for those in search of rare alpine plants. Obviously there is some duplication here, with the same trails appearing repeatedly in book after book after book. Each description, however, is different in some way, shape or form. It all depends on the particular focus of the guidebook.

The use of guidebooks by White Mountains explorers goes back to the second half of the 19th century when interest in the region began to boom with the introduction of passenger railroad service. The railroad companies themselves jumped right into the competitive guidebook market by producing tourist guides of their own.

The first true White Mountains hiking guidebook was authored by Moses Foster Sweetser, who in 1876 penned *The White Mountains: A Handbook for Travellers.* This "stout, handsome, red-jacketed book," as it is described by authors Guy and Laura Waterman in their exhaustive 1989 study of the history of hiking in the Northeast, for the first time provided route descriptions to most of the region's major summits.

Sweetser's book, which went through many editions before finally going out of print in the early 1900s, ranks No. 1 on my list as the best White Mountains guidebook ever produced. Not only does it provide insight into the early development of trails throughout the region, but it also allows a glimpse back into life in the White Mountains in the latter half of the 19th century, with information on area communities, railroad train schedules, and local hotel accommodations.

One of the major highlights of Sweetser's work was the inclusion of fold-out panoramic views from six different summits, including Mount Washington, Mount Prospect, and Jefferson Hill. These view guides amply supplemented Sweetser's text which was heavy on summit view descriptions.

Unlike today's trail guides, which focus more on trail descriptions and less on what you see once you reach the mountaintop, Sweetser's guidebook pandered to those looking for a "peak with a view." His chapter on Mount Washington, which includes the panoramic view, also devotes 11 pages of text to the summit vista!

[It's good to see that in just the last month or so, a new White Mountains guide with similar panoramic views has been published. *Scudder's White Mountain Viewing Guide* by Brent E. Scudder was published last month and signals a return, of sorts, to the most popular guidebook of a century ago.]

The perils of mountain tramping were also aptly covered in Sweetser's guidebook, though it could be argued he went overboard in some instances.

"The traveller among the deep forests and uninhabited glens is apt to meet terrible and pitiless enemies in the form of black flies and mosquitoes," wrote Sweetser. "They come in such vast numbers, and with such unappeasable hunger, that it is almost impossible to keep them away for a moment, and their stings are so sharp and empoisoned as to wellnigh madden their unfortunate victims."

As Sweetser's guide has been long out-of-print, it is not easy to find a useable, readable copy. The going price for early editions of his book is in the $50–60 range. Later, inferior editions of his book are more plentiful and come cheaper, but they lack the depth and significance of the first couple of editions.

While it is no longer practical to carry an outdated Sweetser guide in one's backpack, it is essential that a hiker lug some sort of modern guidebook along. It matters not whether it's the revered *AMC White Mountain Guide*, or one of Dan Doan's classic *Fifty Hikes* books, just as long as it's accurate and up-to-date.

Guidebooks are trailside and bedside companions whose value should never be underestimated. They deserve space right alongside that extra pair of wool socks, that small bottle of bug dope, and that baggie full of gorp.

The ABC's
of the White Mountains

August 23, 1995

With another school year just about upon us, it's only fitting that I use this space today to review the ABC's of the White Mountains.

In alphabetical order, here's a list of some names, places and faces frequently visited or often associated with this wonderful area of northern New England.

APPALACHIAN TRAIL   This 2,160-mile long distance hiking trail connects Springer Mountain in Georgia with Mount Katahdin in northern Maine. The section of the AT that passes through the White Mountains is considered just about the toughest on the entire trail.

BONDCLIFF (MOUNT)   A 4,265-foot peak in the heart of the Pemigewasset Wilderness, this mountain is about the most inaccessible high peak in the region, being more than nine miles from the nearest road. Its rocky, open summit has a commanding view of the nearby East Branch country and an intimate perspective on its sister peaks, Mount Bond and West Bond.

CRAWFORD NOTCH   Historically, perhaps the most significant of all the great notches of the White Mountains. It was here that tourism in the region originated with the efforts of early innkeepers Abel Crawford and his son, Ethan Allen Crawford.

DRY RIVER   Also known as the Mount Washington River, this river flows south out of Oakes Gulf and into Crawford Notch, where it enjoins the Saco River just south of the Crawford Notch State Park boundary.

EISENHOWER (MOUNT)   For many years known as Mount Pleasant, this round-topped mountain in the southern Presidential Range is the 11th highest peak in the region at 4,761 feet. It was renamed in honor of President Dwight D. Eisenhower in 1972.

FRANCONIA NOTCH   Long known for its scenic splendor, this great mountain pass is home to natural wonders such as the Flume, the Basin, and New Hampshire's state symbol, the Old Man of the Mountain. It's also one heck of a place to be during a winter storm, when the wind is howling, the snow is falling, and traffic is crawling at a snail's pace.

GREENLEAF HUT   One of the Appalachian Mountain Club's famous backcountry huts, this hut is situated on a shoulder of Mount Lafayette at about 4,200-foot elevation, and is accessible via the Old Bridle Path or Greenleaf Trail out of Franconia Notch.

HANCOCK (NORTH AND SOUTH PEAKS)   The last of the great unexplored 4,000-footers, these two mountaintops were rarely visited by hikers until the completion of the Kancamagus Highway several decades ago. The north peak is scarred by a huge slide on its south face. The south summit is mostly wooded, but a decent view to the southeast is obtained from a lookout a few yards down off the mountaintop.

ISOLATION (MOUNT)   Despite its name, this 4,005-foot peak south of Mount Washington is not as isolated as one may think. The Davis Path hiking trail, which dates back to the mid-19th century, passes near its open summit. Mount Isolation is best known for its view into Washington's spectacular south-facing Oakes Gulf.

JEWELL TRAIL   A popular approach trail from the west to Mount Washington, this footpath begins off the Base Road, about a mile below the Cog Railway's base station. The trail terminates at the Gulfside Trail, about 1.5 miles below Washington's summit.

KING RAVINE   Named for 19th-century writer Rev. Thomas Starr King, this is the huge glacial cirque on the north side of Mount Adams. The floor of the ravine is noted for its huge boulders, through which pass several hiking trails.

The summit vista from North Hancock is highlighted by the view south toward Mount Osceola.

LAFAYETTE (MOUNT)   Next to Mount Washington, perhaps the most popular peak to climb in the White Mountains. At 5,260-foot, it's the highest peak outside of the Presidentials.

MARSHFIELD STATION   Since 1869, the Mount Washington Cog Railway has been operating from this area at the western base of the northeast's highest mountain. It is named jointly for Sylvester Marsh, inventor of the Cog Railway, and Darby Field, Washington's first conqueror in 1642.

NORTH FORK JUNCTION   The spot where the North Fork and the East Branch of the Pemigewasset River meet. It's also the southern terminus of the Thoreau Falls Trail from Zealand Notch.

OLD MAN OF THE MOUNTAIN   The Great Stone Face, high above Profile Lake in Franconia Notch. Undisputedly New Hampshire's most senior citizen.

PRESIDENTIAL RANGE   The White Mountains region's most spectacular and popular mountain ridge. It runs north to south and includes the five highest peaks in the state: Mounts Washington, Adams, Jefferson, Monroe and Madison.

QUIMBY'S PILLOW   A 500-pound boulder near Mount Moriah's summit, named for Prof. E.T. Quimby, who occupied the mountain's summit in 1879 at one of the stations of the U.S. Coast and Geodetic Survey.

RANDOLPH PATH   Constructed about 100 years ago by pioneer trailbuilder J. Rayner Edmands, this trail traverses the lower slopes of Mounts Madison and Adams, joining the Gulfside Trail in Edmands Col. The last 0.6 mile are above treeline and can be nasty in times of foul weather.

SIGNAL RIDGE   An open, spur ridge just below the summit of Mount Carrigain, from which stunning views are obtained of nearby Carrigain Notch and the distant peaks of the Presidentials.

TUCKERMAN RAVINE   The most famous glacial cirque in the Whites, it is synonymous with daredevil spring skiing, and far too often, tragedy. Skiers and climbers alike have met their deaths in this bowl on the southeast flank of Mount Washington.

UNKNOWN POND   A North Country gem far off the beaten path of most trampers. It can be reached via the Kilkenny Ridge Trail or the Unknown Pond Trail near the Berlin Fish Hatchery on York Pond Road.

VOSE SPUR   A sub peak of Mount Carrigain, this 3,870-foot peak on the Lincoln-Livermore town line is trailless, but is often climbed by bushwhackers seeking to reach New England's 100 Highest mountains.

WASHINGTON (MOUNT)   At 6,288 feet, this is the granddaddy peak of New England and the Northeast. So much has already been written about this mountain, why bother to add even more?

YORK POND   A northern White Mountains pond and site of the

The Old Man of the Mountain looks out over the Pemigewasset River valley and Franconia Notch from his lofty perch high up on Cannon Mountain.

Berlin Fish Hatchery. Its access road is used primarily by hikers bent on exploring the Kilkenny District mountains.

Zealand Valley   An area of the National Forest once ravaged by timber operations and subsequent forest fires, this valley has remarkably regenerated into one of the most diverse, scenic spots in all the White Hills.

What's In a
White Mountains Name?

November 22, 1995

A glance at any good map of the White Mountains region will reveal dozens of interesting names for various mountaintops, ponds and lakes, rivers, and other geographic features.

Many of these names have roots to the region's storied past as they either honor some early settler or mountain explorer. Others bear more descriptive names, chosen as a result of some obvious physical characteristic.

The Crawford Notch area, for instance, is named for the famous Crawford family that nearly two centuries ago inhabited the region between present day Bretton Woods and the Notchland Inn.

Ethan Pond, at the western base of Mount Willey, is named for Ethan Allen Crawford, the so-called 19th-century "Giant of the Hills," whose exploits have been well chronicled in many White Mountains books.

The Crawford Path, which runs from the top of the Notch to the summit of Mount Washington, is named for its trail builders, Abel and Ethan Allen Crawford.

There's also 3,129-foot Mount Crawford, a peak several miles south of the actual Notch, and 4,047-foot Mount Tom, named for Ethan's brother Tom, longtime proprietor of the Notch House near the narrow Gateway of the Notch.

Not everything in the Notch is named for the Crawfords, of course. Take, for example, the infamous Elephant Head rock formation at the Gateway to the Notch. For obvious reasons (especially to those looking up at the rock from the Saco Lake area), it got its name for its striking resemblance to an elephant's head.

Ripley Falls, an 80-foot waterfall on Avalanche Brook at the south end of Mount Willey, is named for a North Conway fisherman who reportedly came across the falls back in 1858. It was the Rev. Thomas Starr King, a famous writer of the era, who suggested the falls bear Ripley's name. Ripley supposedly played the name game himself, renaming the brook on which the falls flow for its proximity to the tragic 1826 landslide that killed Sam Willey and his family during a drenching August rainstorm. The brook was formerly known as Cow Brook.

Being a longtime mountain climber and peakbagger, I've always found the mountaintop nomenclature to be particularly interesting, especially when it comes to the 4,000-foot peaks of the White Mountains.

Several of the high peaks bear the names of famous Indians—some with ties to the region, others with no ties at all.

Mount Passaconaway in the Sandwich Range is named for the powerful 17th century chieftain of New Hampshire's Penacook confederation, while Mount Osceola in the Waterville Valley region is named for a Seminole indian chief who fought for the U.S. Army in Florida. Osceola didn't always bear the chief's name, however. It was originally known as Mad River Peak, in honor of the mountain stream that passes below and through the beautiful Waterville Valley.

The Carter Range on the western side of Pinkham Notch has an interesting story behind its naming. Carter Dome and its neighboring peaks (South, Middle and North Carter) are, at least according to some accounts, named for Dr. Ezra Carter, a Concord physician and botanist who in the early part of the 19th century frequented the White Mountains region, reportedly in search of roots and herbs, which he used for medicinal purposes. Mount Hight, a 4,675-foot subpeak less than a mile north of the Dome, is supposedly named for a frequent hiking companion of Dr. Carter, a Mr. Hight of Jefferson.

Other accounts, however, say the two mountains were actually named for two local trappers (named Carter and Hight) who lost their way and wound up climbing to the summits of the two different peaks in the Carter range. Guidebook author Moses F. Sweetser wrote in early editions of his 19th century guide that it is uncertain which man climbed which peak, but that the mountain west of Carter Notch was usually referred to as Mount Hight, and the peak east of the notch, Mount Carter. The western peak is known today as Wildcat Mountain, while the name Mount Hight has been given to the rocky, pointed peak that is Carter Dome's closest neighbor to the north.

Among the other high summits of the Whites which have undergone name changes over the years are Mounts Garfield, Pierce, Eisenhower, and Hancock.

Garfield was first known as Hooket, and then Haystack. Its name was permanently changed by Franconia selectmen in 1881 when President James Garfield was assassinated.

Mount Pierce, meanwhile, has long endured an identity crisis as it has commonly been known both as Mount Pierce and Mount Clinton. As a result of an act of the New Hampshire legislature on April 13, 1903, the mountain's official name is Mount Pierce, in honor of the nation's 14th President, New Hampshire native Franklin Pierce. The peak's original name—in honor of former New York governor and senator DeWitt Clinton (1769–1828)—has continued to live on, however, thanks greatly to the Appalachian Mountain Club, which for more than 70 years continued to list the Mount Clinton name on all its hiking maps. It wasn't until the mid-1970s that AMC finally relented and tagged the summit with both names on its hiking maps. For the record, AMC maps now found in the club's popular *White Mountain Guide* identify the mountain as Pierce, with Clinton listed in parentheses. Other mapmakers haven't been as accommodating, though, and still insist on using just the mountain's original name.

As for Mount Hancock, it was first known as Pemigewasset Peak —no doubt due to its proximity to the East Branch of the Pemigewasset River.

Mount Eisenhower is the most recently renamed 4,000-footer. It was just 23 years ago, in 1972, that the mountain was christened in name of former President Dwight Eisenhower. Prior to that it was called Mount Pleasant, and before that Dome Mountain.

A Top Notch Quiz

July 31, 1996

In other parts of the country they are known as passes, or gaps, but here in the White Mountains of New Hampshire we have our own term for these cuts or wedges between the mountains. They are called Notches—a term pegged by early settlers of the region who compared the sharp mountain defiles to the wedges or notches they so often employed while cutting down trees for firewood or for building material.

Certainly most everyone is familiar with at least some of the Notches which are spread about the White Mountains. Franconia Notch will forever be linked with New Hampshire's trademark Old Man of the Mountain while Pinkham Notch is nearly synonymous with Mount Washington, Tuckerman Ravine and the Appalachian Mountain Club.

There are more to these notches than just their names, of course, so this week I thought I'd offer up a little quiz so readers could find out for themselves just how much they know about our many White Mountains notches.

1. There are more notches around these hills than one would probably surmise. Using a White Mountain National Forest map as my source, I've identified 24 such notches. How many can you name?

2. The valley leading from the north into this particular notch was once home to what one late 19th-century writer termed "the crookedest . . . and steepest" logging railroad line in New England. Through what notch did this railroad run?

3. Willard and Bunnell Notch are considered the White Mountains region's two most northerly notches, both being situated in the isolated Kilkenny mountains north of Route 2. Which White Mountains notches are furthest to the south, east and west?

4. Most hikers headed into this rugged White Mountains notch will trek in from the west, but it's also easily accessed from the southeast by the lesser used Wildcat River Trail. What Notch is this?

5. Carrigain Notch is one of the central White Mountains region's most wild, uncivilized notches. The two peaks towering high above its valley floor on each side are wild as well, neither being accessible by footpath. Which two peaks frame Carrigain Notch?

6. Crawford Notch is famous for its namesake pioneer innkeepers who once inhabited this region, the infamous 1826 landslide that killed the Willey family, and the railroad line that climbs up through the notch at the base of Mounts Willey and Willard. Lesser known are some of its interesting natural features, like Kedron Flume on the side of Mount Willey and Frankenstein Cliff at the south end of the notch. Can you name Crawford Notch's other notable "flume," or perhaps the four major water-falls frequented so often by hikers and passing motorists?

7. Which high mountain notch is crossed by the state's most elevated public through road?

8. A string of eight beaver ponds dot the floor of this hidden mountain pass in the southwest recesses of the WMNF. Dig deep to come up with the answer.

9. I'd be willing to bet that most White Mountains hikers have never been to, or even heard of Carlton Notch. In fact, there are two such notches in the region. Where exactly are these pair of unknown notches?

10. You can search and search for this eastern White Mountains notch, but it might take a while to find this one on your map.

11. Nineteenth-century writer Rev. Thomas Starr King once wrote of this famous White Mountains notch, "The narrow district thus enclosed contains more objects of interest to the mass of travelers than any other region of equal extant within the usual compass of the White Mountains tour." State Parks officials would no doubt agree.

A string of beaver ponds, like the one seen above, dot the landscape in Tunnel Ravine or Tunnel Notch, one of the area's least visited notches.

12. Up until trail builders cut paths to this notch's namesake summits a few decades ago, it's likely the notch itself got more traffic than its 4,000-foot peaks.

Answers

1. Albany Notch, Bear Notch, Bunnell Notch, Carlton Notch (two actually), Carrigain Notch, Carter Notch, Crawford Notch, Dickey Notch, Evans Notch, Franconia Notch, Jefferson Notch, Kinsman Notch, Hancock Notch, Haystack Notch, Mad River Notch, Miles Notch, Oliverian Notch, Perkins Notch, Pinkham Notch, Sandwich Notch, Tyler Notch, Willard Notch, and Zealand Notch. One might also include Mahoosuc and Grafton Notches in far western Maine as being among the White Mountains notches, while some people also refer to the pass between Mount Clough and Mount Moosilauke in Easton as Tunnel Brook Notch, though it doesn't appear that way on my WMNF map. One could also argue that Jakes and White Notches, both situated in the eastern Mahoosucs of Maine, should be included here as they appear on the WMNF map, but technically aren't in the White Mountains.

2. Zealand Notch, where J. E. Henry's Zealand Valley logging railroad operated for about a dozen years in the 1880s and 1890s.

3. Furthest south is Sandwich Notch, made famous by Elizabeth Yeats' historical novel, *The Road Through Sandwich Notch*. Furthest east is Albany Notch in western Maine, near the Crocker Pond area. Oliverian Notch in the Warren-Benton area is the westernmost notch and is passed through by Route 25 between East Haverhill and Warren.

4. Carter Notch, home to one of AMC's older backcountry huts. The Wildcat River Trail is reached by driving to the end of Carter Notch Road in Jackson.

5. Vose Spur, a 3,862-foot peak just east of Mount Carrigain, forms the west wall of the notch. To the east is 3,743-foot Mount Lowell.

6. Hitchcock Flume on Mount Willard's eastern slope is accessible via a side trail a short distance down from the summit. (Some old maps also cite Butterwort Flume and Tilted Flume as being situated on Mount Willard's west slopes, but as far as I know, neither is accessible by trail). The four popular waterfalls in Crawford Notch include the roadside Silver Cascade and Flume Cascade, plus Ripley Falls on Avalanche Brook and Arethusa Falls on Bemis Brook.

7. Jefferson Notch, with an elevation of just over 3,000 feet, is traversed by Jefferson Notch Road, which connects the Cog Railway Base Road with Route 2 in the Jefferson–Randolph area.

8. Tunnel Brook Notch, long a popular destination for fisherman.

9. Carlton Notch in Randolph passes between Mount Crescent and Mount Randolph. There's also a Carlton Notch that straddles the Maine–N.H. border in the Shelburne–Wild River area.

10. Haystack Notch passes between Haystack Mountain and Butters Mountain in the Caribou–Speckled Mountain Wilderness Area of western Maine.

11. Franconia Notch, undoubtedly the most visited of all the great White Mountains notches.

12. Hancock Notch, which separates the peaks of the Hancock Range from trailless Mount Huntington.

Eight Things You Might Not Know About the White Mountains

November 13, 1997

1. Peakbaggers today know all about New Hampshire's forty-eight 4,000-foot summits, which range in elevation from 6,288-foot Mount Washington to 4,003-foot Mount Tecumseh. But many of today's hikers probably aren't aware that the first person to compose a list of the high peaks of the White Mountains was Dartmouth College librarian, Prof. N. L. Goodrich, who in 1931 published a list of 36 peaks he felt area climbers might feel compelled to ascend.

Goodrich figured that since climbers elsewhere in the world (and even in the U.S.) were into climbing mountains of a certain elevation, New England climbers should have their own list of peaks as well.

The practice of attaining the peaks on certain lists, "Appears to drive men up mountains they would otherwise neglect," wrote Goodrich in an article in *Appalachia* journal.

His original list of peaks did not include summits like North Twin, South Carter, Willey, North Kinsman, Bondcliff, and several others, primarily because they did not meet his qualifications of having a minimum 300-foot rise above the low point of the mountain's connecting ridge with a higher neighbor.

He speculated that at least one person had climbed all the peaks on his list, but he could not confirm that suspicion.

2. Mount Bondcliff, the remote 4,265-foot peak at the south end of the Twin–Bond Range, was the last peak to be added to the New Hampshire 4,000-footer list. The peak was added in 1980 after it was determined that the rise from its low point in the col south of neigh-

boring Mount Bond to its summit was greater than 200 feet, which by then was the peakbagging standard.

The fact that the peak is a late addition to the list is apropos as Bondcliff was also one of the last major peaks in the region to have a trail cut to its summit. Up until the mid-1920s, few trampers ever walked across Bondcliff's dramatic ledgy summit as the closest footpath ended on the summit of Mount Bond. Early AMC guidebooks warned of the treachery involved in a bushwhack hike to Bondcliff from its northern neighbor. "The distance is not over ½ mile, but there is no path and the way is made all but impassable by the continuous breast-high scrub," warned AMC in the 1920 edition of its guide.

Devoted AMC trailblazer Karl Harrington is credited with cutting the first path to Bondcliff sometime in the mid-1920s. Previously, hikers atop Mount Bond bypassed Bondcliff on their ascents or descents by utilizing a woods path that connected Bond's summit with the area near North Fork junction on the East Branch of the Pemigewasset River.

3. Overnight visitors to Lonesome Lake in Franconia Notch formerly paid to stay in shoreline cabins built in 1876 by the lake's discoverer, 19th-century writer and fishing enthusiast William C. Prime.

The primitive cabins—described in one guidebook as "quaint, woodland" cottages—stood at the north end of the lake and for more than 30 years were maintained by AMC as a precursor to present-day Lonesome Lake Hut. The state of New Hampshire, after buying the land around the lake in late 1928, leased the cabins to AMC until 1963, when the state constructed a new building at the south end of the mountain tarn. AMC leased that building (now the hut), and eventually purchased it outright in 1979.

4. The round summit that towers high above Lonesome Lake's north shore—4,100-foot Cannon Mountain—has been known by several names over the years, including Profile, Freak and Old Man's Mountain. But its permanent moniker has no relationship at all to the mountain's most famous landmark, the Old Man of the Mountain.

Instead, the Cannon referenced in the mountain's name is an oblong rock near the mountain's summit that from a distance, resembles a cannon.

In year's past, a rough footpath leading to "the cannon" from the Kinsman Ridge Trail could be followed. No mention of this trail has appeared in guidebooks for decades, however, and no signs of any footway are evident atop the heavily forested summit ridge.

5. Spectacular Mount Carrigain, a peak long known for its outstanding summit vista, was first climbed on August 27, 1857 by Swiss scientist Arnold Henri Guyot and his party of explorers. Guyot, who is well-known for his early study of glaciers, is credited with proving to the world that Mount Washington was not the highest peak east of the Mississippi River, as was commonly believed a century and a half ago.

The ascent route of Guyot and his party is unknown, but in their book *Forest and Crag*, authors Laura and Guy Waterman speculate the Guyot party probably bushwhacked from Carrigain Notch up the steep flank of Vose Spur. From there they passed over another intermediate hump along the ridge and finally made it to Carrigain's 4,680-foot summit in four hours time with "scratched face and hands, bruised feet, and well-torn clothes."

6. The imposing west-facing slope of 4,832-foot Carter Dome— ninth highest mountain in New Hampshire—was forever scarred in October 1869 when a drenching rainstorm caused a massive mile-long landslide that stripped the mountain slope to its bedrock.

Forty-four years later, disaster struck the mountain again when a ferocious fire ravaged its ridgeline, denuding much of the mountain of its vegetation, including its spur peak, Mount Hight.

A wooden fire lookout stand at Carter Dome's summit was even a victim of the mountain firestorm.

7. Speaking of natural disasters, the infamous Hurricane of 1938 laid to waste much of the land in and around the White Mountains.

In Crawford Notch, huge stands of virgin softwood timber were leveled by the September 21 storm. These stands were situated in the area of the Mount Field–Tom col and near Nancy Pond.

The just completed Nancy Pond Trail, open less than six months, was made impassable by the ruins of the hurricane. It would be 22 years before the trail was reopened.

Meanwhile at the top of the Notch, the reconstructed carriage road to Mount Willard—given a complete overhaul in the years previous to the storm by Civilian Conservation Corps workers—was pretty much laid to waste by the torrential rains which accompanied the storm.

Elsewhere in the mountains, the Forest Service claimed 175 million board feet of merchantable timber were knocked down by heavy winds accompanying the storm—including a stand of more virgin timber along Breadtray Ridge near Mount Osceola.

In Franconia Notch, two landslides, one near the "Old Man" lookout, buried the Notch road under 10–15 feet of debris. AMC's Greenleaf Hut, on a shoulder of Mount Lafayette, was also left isolated by the storm. The Greenleaf Trail was reported to be "completely obliterated by fallen trees and more than a half dozen slides" and the "impassable tangle on the Garfield Ridge" cut off the approach to the hut by way of Mount Lafayette.

8. Mount Field, the highest peak in the Willey Range near Crawford Notch, was originally named in honor of one of America's greatest presidents, Abraham Lincoln.

But upon publication in 1871 of his epic *Geology of New Hampshire*, state geologist Charles Hitchcock bestowed the name of Mount Field on the 4,326-foot mountain in honor of Darby Field, the first white man to reach Mount Washington's summit 1642.

Hitchcock's rationale for the name change was reasonable as he noted that a peak in the Franconia range already bore Lincoln's name. In order to avoid unnecessary confusion, a name change was in order, he prescribed.

This Peakbagging Pup
Doesn't Dog It on the Trail

December 4, 1996

Five-and-a-half month old "Scooter" Ruiter–McIntyre makes no bones about it. By this time next year, he intends to be among the youngest, if not the youngest dog ever to have attained all 48 of New Hampshire's 4,000-foot summits.

The handsome border collie, who climbed his first major White Mountain summit a mere nine weeks ago, is more than a quarter of the way toward finishing off the hallowed 4,000-footer peakbagging list. With 13 official summits already to his credit, and the prospect of several more hikes on the horizon between now and the start of the new year, it's conceivable, Scooter thinks, that he could be up to 20 summits by the start of the New Year.

Scooter was "born to hike" according to his two co-owners, Creston Ruiter and Alan McIntyre of Whitefield. Ruiter, an accomplished peakbagger himself, accompanies the dog on most of his climbs, and in the two months since joining Scooter for a September 28 ascent of 4,054-foot Mount Hale, he can already sense that Scooter has been bitten by the contagious peakbagging bug.

Although still just a pup, Scooter already acts and sounds like a veteran canine tramper. He knows all about crampons, and switchbacks, and above treeline travel. He sticks close to his hiking companions, no matter how slow they may be walking. And he appreciates a good summit vista and a middle of the hiking day cookie break.

Scooter was born on June 17 of this year and came into the hands of Ruiter and McIntyre seven weeks later. By the time he was nine weeks old, he was climbing his first mountains. Then a few days after he turned three months old, he led Ruiter up to Mount Hale's semi-open summit, where he got his first taste of real White Mountain hiking.

Like most dogs, Scooter travels faster than his human hiking mates, but realizing he has a lot to learn yet about the ways of the woods, he's cautious about getting too far ahead of his party.

"I like to roam some while I'm on the trail, but not that much. I'm still just a shy little thing, so when I realize I'm approaching someone else on the trail, I run back to Cres or Alan and they put me back on a leash," explained the dog in a recent interview. "I'm not one to hound other hikers. I respect the backcountry hiking experience and those who are there to enjoy it."

On one of his earliest backwoods hikes, Scooter says he experienced one of the more harrowing incidents of his young life. "There I was, minding my own business, sniffing my way along the Mount Willard Trail, when this big bully of a dog comes at me and attacks for no justifiable reason. Ever since then I've been leery about meeting other furry-faced creatures—canine or human. I guess that's why I'm so agreeable to being hooked to a leash. It gives me a sense of security," said the dog.

Scooter generally travels light when he heads into the high country. "I let the humans do the dirty work," he freely admits. "They carry extra water for me, especially when we've planned a hike on a trail that tends to be dry. And they get to lug my trail and snack foods. You'll never catch me wearing a fanny pack. Not with these humans so willing to carry my load."

On a typical hike, he'll consume whatever water he can find, plus the usual ration of dog biscuits and dried dog foods. "I've been known to take handouts from other hikers too, but generally Creston and Alan discourage me from eating human food."

The summits Scooter has visited thus far vary in difficulty from Mount Hale and Mount Jackson—two of the easier 4,000-footers—to 5,367-foot Mount Madison in the northern Presidentials. He's also hiked in varying amounts of snow and ice, and his longest trek was an early October traverse of the Zealand–Twin Ranges—a trip that covered 14.5 miles and included ascents of three 4,000-footers.

"That was definitely my toughest day. First I fell in the Gale River when we were headed up to North Twin. Then we ran into some snow, ice and mud up on the ridge. By the time we got to Mount

Guyot and ran into this group of hikers that Creston knew, I was ready for a nice long nap. It was only then that I learned I still had another six or seven miles to go. I wasn't real happy or very sociable at that point."

Being a dog, perhaps it's only natural that Scooter prefers the heavily forested summits over the open, airy mountaintops that human hikers value. In Scooter's case, the more trees to leave his calling card with, the better. "Mount Zealand doesn't find much favor with you humans, but I really got my kicks out of that place. I liked it so much that after Creston and I hiked to the official summit area and walked back to the Twinway trail, I convinced him to let me off the lease so I could go back and hit it again. I was hoping the second visit would count for my next round of 48. Now I'm told it doesn't. Oh well, guess I'll have to go back again next year."

Scooter's list of conquered peaks includes Mounts Hale, Zealand, the Twins, Field, Tom, Willey, Cabot, Waumbek, Jackson, Eisenhower and Clinton. Of the latter summit, Scooter says he'll always be a traditionalist and not call the mountain by its official name (Mount Pierce). ["Some things were meant to stay the same," he argues, "and the Mount Clinton name is one of those things."]

When the peakbagging bug first hit him hard in mid-October, after he'd reached his seventh or eighth summit, he admits he had visions of getting half the peaks done by the end of the year, and the remaining 24 between January 1 and his first birthday next June.

"The goal of reaching 24 peaks by December 31 is definitely out of the question, but there's no reason why I can't get a few more summits in between now and New Year's, especially now that much of our early snow has been washed away," he said.

As for finishing all the peaks by June 17, well that will depend a lot on the winter and spring hiking conditions, and the enthusiasm and health of his human hiking mates.

"Let's face it, without them, I don't get very far. They drive me to the trailheads. They read the maps for me. They carry all of my food. I can only go as far as they'll take me. If they're not in the mood, then I'm plumb out of luck.

"I hope that never happens, though, because I've gotten to see a lot more of the mountains than my brothers and sisters. I'll tell you one thing. The first time Creston or Al tell me they're not in the mood to go hiking, they'll be the ones in the doghouse, not me."

About the Author

Mike Dickerman has been reporting on news events in the White Mountains of New Hampshire for more than a decade as a staff member with the weekly newspaper, *The Courier* of Littleton, N.H. His popular hiking column, "The Beaten Path," earned him New Hampshire Press Association Sports Columnist of the Year honors in 1995. He is currently sports editor with *The Courier*, and his previous books include *Along the Beaten Path* and *A Guide to Crawford Notch* (coauthored by Steven D. Smith and John Dickerman). Mike lives in Littleton with his wife, Jeanne.